AGASSI

THE FALL AND RISE OF THE
ENFANT TERRIBLE OF TENNIS
ROBERT PHILIP

BLOOMSBURY

For Sue

Acknowledgement

With special thanks to Richard Evans and to Michael Cole, a wonderful photographer and a dreadful friend.

First published 1993
This paperback edition first published 1994 by
Bloomsbury Publishing Ltd, 2 Soho Square, London W1V 5DE
Copyright © by Robert Philip 1993, 1994
The moral right of the author has been asserted

A CIP catalogue record for this book is available from the
British Library

ISBN 07475 1451 8

Typeset by Hewer Text Composition Services, Edinburgh
Printed and bound in Britain by Cox & Wyman Ltd, Reading, Berks

Contents

1

Game, Set and Match

Andre Agassi was playing like an angel and behaving like a choirboy.

Boris Becker had been mastered in the quarter-finals and a rejuvenated John McEnroe overwhelmed in the semis. Now the twenty-two-year-old Nevadan stood just one tantalising point away from becoming the 1992 Wimbledon champion as Goran Ivanisevic prepared to serve and a cathedral-like hush gradually descended upon 13,000 spellbound spectators on the Centre Court.

The towering Croatian rocket launcher had already blasted 206 aces past his seven opponents during the preceding fortnight, but on this occasion his 130 mph first serve screamed well wide of the target zone. When his nervously struck second delivery scraped over the net with almost apologetic acquiescence, Agassi took three steps forward and struck a fizzing double-fisted backhand which the lunging Ivanisevic could return only as far as the bottom of the net. What will be remembered as one of the most captivating Wimbledon finals of the modern era was over.

Umpire John Frame's rich Scottish tones proclaiming, 'Game, set and match, Agassi . . . 6–7, 6–4, 6–4, 1–6, 6–4,' were largely lost amid the rising crescendo of noise as the new champion slumped to his knees then collapsed spreadeagled on the sacred grass, tears of joy, relief and wonderment streaming down his stubbled cheeks. The gallant Ivanisevic climbed over the net as in days of yore to embrace his conqueror and whisper privately: 'You deserve it, man. You played great all these two weeks.'

After a roller-coaster six-year career during which he had come to be seen as a sporting god by some, and as a money-making monster by others, Agassi, from that instant on, became a global superstar, as immediately recognisable to all as Prince or Pavarotti.

'Image,' he once proclaimed in an advertising commercial for a camera-maker which would frequently come back to haunt him, 'is everything.' But despite the peroxide-blond pony-tail, the three-day growth on his chin, the earrings, the nail varnish, the on-court affectations and the kaleidoscope wardrobe, the sharpest image presented by this kid from Las Vegas – until that Sunday afternoon in 1992 – was that of a born loser created by some fiendish mind on Madison Avenue.

Three times he had contested – and lost – major finals in Paris and New York, to Andres Gomez, Pete Sampras and Jim Courier, thereby earning a reputation for being prone to stage-fright; and after his humiliating defeat by Frenchman Henri Leconte on his 1987 debut appearance at Wimbledon he had become so uncertain of his ability to adapt to grass courts that he had come up with all manner of lame excuses for three successive years to avoid the All England Club. Now, in only his thirteenth match on grass, Agassi, the man his vociferous band of critics noisily claimed would never win any of the four Grand Slam tennis championships, had gained the greatest prize of all.

'You might find this a strange thing for me to say, but I remember feeling kinda sad afterwards,' recalls Agassi. 'Tennis had always given my life so much, and now Wimbledon had given my life so much, it's a real shame I didn't come to respect it a little earlier. I suppose it's ironic after all the disappointments

I'd suffered in the French and US championships, that I should then achieve my greatest triumph at Wimbledon. I'd had a lot of chances to fulfil a lot of dreams in the past and never succeeded. To do it at Wimbledon, which is the spiritual home of tennis, is more than I could have ever asked for. If my career was to end right here and now, I think I've got a lot more than any one person deserves from life.

'It was probably only around Christmas that I had time to sit down on my own back home in Las Vegas and really think about last summer's Wimbledon, to let what had happened slowly sink in. Most players don't realise – at least I certainly didn't – what being the Wimbledon champion exactly means. In the immediate aftermath of victory, you feel so many emotions, but you don't have any clear concept of just what it is you've actually accomplished. Now, the further I withdraw from that fabulous Sunday all those months ago the more I realise that being the Wimbledon champion just goes on and on and on. It never changes. You are always the Wimbledon champion, now and for ever.'

This unbridled enthusiasm for the hallowed green lawns of London SW19 was in stark contrast to Agassi's attitude two years previously when the All England Club chairman John Curry had flown to Paris in an admirable attempt to arrange a *tête-à-tête* with the self-styled rebel during the 1990 French Open championship to discuss the American's reluctance to show his famous face. 'I just wanted Andre to know that we would do whatever we could to make him comfortable,' proffers Curry by way of explanation. But Curry was never given the opportunity of persuading Wimbledon's most notable absentee to change his mind . . . Agassi refused to grant the chairman an audience. 'I was wrong to stay away,' admits the new champion now. 'I never fully appreciated just how special it feels to walk out on to the Centre Court.'

The image of Agassi clutching the Wimbledon trophy to his chest with all the unrestrained love and disbelief of a child hugging its first puppy will linger in the memory of millions around the world, but, almost inevitably in the face of all that had gone before, there was a trace of controversy in his moment of triumph; he incurred the wrath of a section of the British nation for neglecting to doff his acceptably white baseball cap to the Duke and Duchess of Kent during the presentation ceremony, whilst an American television company offered visual evidence that his joyous celebrations had been carefully stage-managed by long-time coach and mentor Nick Bollettieri from his seat in the VIP box. A video recording appeared to show Agassi falling to his knees at the end of the final before he caught sight of Bollettieri frantically indicating he should adopt the flat-on-the-back pose so irresistible to magazine and newspaper photographers.

The *New York Post* called this inconsequential deception (if, indeed, deception it was) 'damning and disgusting', but even now Agassi firmly refuses to be drawn into a fulsome explanation of his motives at the time in question: 'I really don't think what happened justifies any comment. Honestly, if I need to clear that up – if people can believe there is anything in that story – then they'll believe anything. If you aren't sure, just watch it again. 'It was very, very emotional out there. When I won I fell to the ground and sobbed. I was totally overwhelmed. There's no way to express what I was feeling. The Australian, the French, the US Opens are all important, but I had just won the greatest title in tennis. For me there never has been, and I suppose there never will be, another day like the day I became Wimbledon champion.'

Nor is it a day Mike Agassi, watching on television in the family home at West Tropicana Avenue, Las Vegas, is likely to forget. 'He made us all cry like babies,' laughs the still-jubilant father, who had finally fulfilled a thirty-year quest to fashion a world champion. 'He just wanted it more than Ivanisevic when it came to the crunch. I guess Andre would have stayed out there till it became dark. No way was he ever going to accept defeat. He had to win. After all, how many chances like that do you get in life?'

Looking back, Agassi can recall the seventy-two hours

immediately following his Wimbledon victory only as a blurred tapestry: the Champions' Ball in dinner suit and bow tie at the Savoy in London's West End with girlfriend Wendy Stewart; celebrating with the newly-crowned ladies' champion Steffi Graf (all beaming smiles and plunging neckline); the flight home to Las Vegas aboard the private jet of close friend and millionaire casino owner Steve Wynn; and his arrival at McCarran International Airport where a group of departing gamblers came to an open-mouthed halt on the tarmac to give him a resounding welcome.

Agassi's new found celebrity attracted attention of an altogether different sort during autumn 1992's US Open at Flushing Meadow, New York (where he was beaten by his bitter rival Jim Courier in the quarter-finals). He was romantically linked with fifty-year-old chanteuse Barbra Streisand after he and the singer-actress-film director were seen embracing following his second-round victory over Dutchman Jan Siemerink. Long-time acquaintances from Las Vegas, Agassi (who has a secret desire to be a film-star) had telephoned Streisand after seeing her latest film, *Prince of Tides*, and rumours of an unlikely affair swept New York when she was spotted at courtside in a floppy white sunhat and a revealing off-the-shoulder white dress. The tabloids chose to ignore that she was flanked by Bollettieri and an obviously star-struck Wendy Stewart.

After she was seen to hand Agassi a gift in a tiny silver box before he played Spain's Carlos Costa, Streisand was prevailed upon to open her heart. She revealed, somewhat enigmatically, it has to be said, that Agassi was 'very evolved, more than his linear years. He's an extraordinary human being. He plays like a Zen master.' For his part, Agassi admitted he had no idea how a Zen master might be expected to play tennis ('I'm going to have to talk to her about that one') and added: 'Some of the things Barbra has done are absolutely amazing. It's a great honour for me to hear she has such a high opinion of me. Of course, it's exciting to have her out there watching. It is the ultimate compliment from someone who has accomplished so much.'

Agassi, too, has accomplished much. He ended 1992 by inspiring the United States to victory over Switzerland in the final of the Davis Cup at Fort Worth, Texas, and moved up to sixth place on the American *Forbes' Magazine* list of highest-earning sportsmen with an annual income of $11 million. Only basketball phenomenon Michael Jordan, former heavyweight boxing champion Evander Holyfield, racing drivers Ayrton Senna and Nigel Mansell and golfing legend Arnold Palmer, earned more.

'Andre's victory at Wimbledon will be great for him and great for us,' confesses Ian Hamilton, tennis marketing director at Nike, who will pay Agassi $20 million over the next ten years to wear their range of clothing. 'Wimbledon is the jackpot.' Indeed, the $265,000 Agassi took home from the All England Club last July was but a trifle compared to the riches in store for him. Bollettieri, who describes his pupil as 'pure gold', estimates the Wimbledon title could be worth around $8 million a year. The details of all his current sponsorship deals are likely to be renegotiated in his favour over this coming summer, but at the moment Agassi is guaranteed an annual $2 million a year from Nike, the same from Belgian racquet manufacturer Donnay, $1.7 million from watchmaker Ebel, $1.3 million from an American food company, $1 million for wearing a particular brand of sunglasses, plus a vast assortment of contracts to promote cameras, breakfast cereals, mineral water, coffee, vitamins, cars, etc. Also there will be on-court earnings of up to $3 million, including exhibitions.

Nike, who now boast a turnover of $3.4 billion, are well pleased with their investment, even though the company's most recognisable client is often accused of resembling an accident in a paint factory. Agassi's trademark 'crop top' shirt, specially designed to ensure that it flies up at the front, revealing a navel only slightly less popular than Madonna's, is known to Nike as the 'rock' 'n roll tennis' label. Jim Courier and David Wheaton by comparison, play 'tuxedo tennis'.

'The whole "Andre look" came about by chance,' explains Hamilton. 'A few years ago John McEnroe told us how he'd love to wear cut-off jeans on court. We made a few sample pairs of denim shorts which John thought were too heavy – but Andre was ready to kill for them. Then came the lycra-liners, which only Andre Agassi could have pulled off, and it's just gone on from there. Andre has put Nike where we are today.'

Strangely, as the money has flooded in – a reported $35 million to date – so Agassi's tastes have subtly changed, even simplified. Gone are the days when his front drive looked like the starting grid at Le Mans, packed with anything up to a dozen Ferraris, Porsches, Lamborghinis and similarly expensive toys. He can even be seen pedalling around Las Vegas on a bicycle on occasion, and his two-storey, two-bedroomed home on the outskirts of the city is modest compared with many on the Spanish Trail Country Club estate. 'Andre's not a money-animal,' insists Bollettieri. 'If he was, he wouldn't be as generous and giving as he is.'

The contents of Agassi's house, however, are typical Las Vegas: a 'games room' dominated by a cinema-sized television screen, assorted videos, slot-machines and computer poker. 'Don't be fooled by that,' continues Bollettieri, firmly quashing the oft-repeated charge that his student is an intellectual pygmy who lacks imagination. 'Never forget there are two kinds of education in this world – the formal education you receive at school or college or university, and the education you can only get out there on the streets. Andre is one of the sharpest street-educated young men I've ever come across. He only has a high school diploma, but his memory, command of language and quickness of thought are remarkable. He has the loyalty of his friends, the love of a good woman, and his Christianity. Even if he had no money, he'd still be wealthy.'

Much of the criticism levelled at Agassi is that he has chosen to surround himself with an entourage which often appears sneering and contemptuous of outsiders, but in private he can be courteous, inquisitive and caring. Nor does he take his honorary membership of the most exclusive tennis club in the world lightly.

One morning shortly before Christmas, the private telephone rang in the members' lounge at the All England Club and the 1992 Wimbledon champion came on the line to say he was in London and enquired if it was convenient for him to drop by for lunch with a few friends. An hour later, accompanied by brother Phil, personal manager Bill Shelton and Wendy Stewart, Agassi walked into the dining room to the spontaneous applause of the thirty members present. After a 'public school' lunch of soup, roast pork and two veg, and bread and butter pudding, he took his group on a leisurely tour of the grounds and museum before making his way out to the Centre Court where he knelt alone with his thoughts and memories.

It all looked so very different compared with the last time Agassi had surveyed the self-same scene: all was quiet as Agassi relived the events of five months earlier. Afterwards, to the delight of his fellow-members, Agassi demonstrated the famous backhand which had accounted for Ivanisevic on championship point, before his party departed as unhurriedly and as unobtrusively as it had arrived.

One seemingly trivial incident on the night of the Champions' Ball in the Savoy showed that he is determined to be as gracious in triumph as he has always been in times of sporting disaster, when his gentlemanly acceptance of defeat has impressed even his most bitter critics. During that celebration dinner, one of the waiters, clutching an autograph book belonging to his tennis-mad son, had surreptitiously approached the new champion sitting beside Steffi Graf at the top table, but the icy stare of the *maître d'* sent him scurrying away. Towards the end of the evening, however, Agassi quietly took the waiter to one side and not only presented him with a signed commemorative menu, but promised him two tickets for the first Monday of the 1993 Wimbledon, when the defending men's singles champion traditionally opens the tournament on the Centre Court.

2

From Tehran to
Las Vegas

Emmanuel Agassi, who had assumed the name 'Mike' on his
arrival in the United States some seven years earlier, slowly
lowered his eyes from the magnificent thirty-feet-high gold-
framed mirrors to the glittering assemblage seated beneath the
shimmering chandeliers in the great banqueting hall of Chicago's
Ambassador Hotel. Though now a waiter who tried hard to keep
his scuffed shoes hidden, he had been a redoubtable tennis
player back home in Iran, and he felt no shame in serving at
a champagne reception honouring the teams of America and
Australia who were to do battle in the 1959 Davis Cup final at
Forest Hills, New York, that coming weekend.

As the poor immigrant passed along the row of great players
with the water jug – Rod Laver . . . Roy Emerson . . . Neale
Fraser . . . Alex Olmedo . . . Earl Bucholz – he offered up a
silent vow in Armenian, the ancient language of his forefathers:
'One day the son of Emmanuel Agassi will play tennis for the
United States of America in the final of the Davis Cup.'

In fact, the 1992 Wimbledon champion's destiny had already

been fashioned many thousands of miles away and many years before . . .

Emmanuel, an Armenian, was born in 1932 in what was then known as Persia and is now known as Iran. His ancestors had originally scratched a living of sorts by raising scrawny livestock on the isolated volcanic slopes of Mount Ararat, the supposed peak on which Noah's ark finally came to rest on dry land after the Flood. Over a period of centuries, the Armenians, forever under threat of massacre from the Ottoman Turks, spread far and wide into what would become the Soviet Union, Persia, Turkey and other parts of the Middle East.

The son of a merchant, the boy grew up in the narrow steamy alleyways of Tehran which then, like now, were a breeding ground of intrigue and political unrest. The dishonest carried swords and knives, and the law-abiding learned to use their fists as a safety precaution.

There were two landmarks in the life of the nine-year-old Emmanuel in 1941: the Allied governments forced the dictatorial Reza Shah Pahlavi, whom they had long suspected of harbouring pro-Nazi sympathies, to abdicate in favour of his son Mohammed Reza Pahlavi (who would sit on the diamond-encrusted Peacock Throne for almost four decades until he fled into exile in 1979 rather than face the revolutionary wrath of the Ayatollah Khomeini) – and he fell in love with the game of tennis.

Although a member of the Armenian Church the youngster used to escape the sun-baked streets of the capital by clambering over the wall of the tree-lined courtyard of the American Mission Church to read or sleep in the cool shade. 'One day I heard this gentle thwack, thwack, thwack and the sound of laughter coming from around the other side of the churchyard. Being naturally inquisitive, like any small boy of that age, I went to have a look and saw my first tennis match. The courts were made out of dried earth, the GIs weren't very good, and I seem to remember their racquets were missing more than a few strings. But I sat there fascinated, secretly watching from behind a tree.'

His presence had not gone unnoticed, however, and the kindly US soldiers gradually befriended their ragamuffin audience, first with gifts of chocolate, chewing-gum and cocoa, later with an old, long-discarded wooden racquet with thick fuse wire for strings and a couple of dog-eared tennis balls worn as smooth as billiard balls. In return, Emmanuel was good-naturedly encouraged to perform the duties of ball boy and groundsman. 'I watered the court and then flattened it with a huge hand-roller. It was hard work because I was so small, but I loved those afternoons with the GIs – especially when they finally allowed me to knock-up with them after they had finished playing. I don't know how or why, but I took to it easily.'

Though the youngster displayed a natural aptitude for the new game, it was as an amateur boxer that he first gained renown. Word of Emmanuel Agassi's prowess with gloves quickly spread. He was regarded as a prodigy in a nation noticeably short of sporting heroes and there was much wild talk of a gold medal when he left Tehran for the very first time in his life to compete at the 1948 Olympic Games in London. It was the seventeen-year-old Iranian's misfortune to fight as a middleweight against the near-invincible Laszlo Papp of Hungary, who would become the professional champion of Europe in the 1960s. Agassi took advantage of his early defeat to catch a District Line underground train out to Southfields tube station, from where he walked south along Wimbledon Park Road to the front gates of the All England Club in Church Road, a mile from the station.

As the luxury limousines, all of which he felt certain must be Rolls-Royces and Bentleys, swept imperiously by, the young boxer daydreamed as he gazed upon the familiar outline of the Centre Court. Some time, far in the future, he would return, and those same gates would swing open to welcome him.

11

Curiously, the favourite to win Wimbledon in that distant summer of 1948 had been the great American Davis Cup player Richard 'Pancho' Gonzales (who, many years in the future, would become Emmanuel Agassi's son-in-law through marrying his eldest daughter Rita), but he decided against entering the 1948 singles championship. When he did play twelve months later (he was then reigning US national champion), he was unexpectedly beaten by Australian Geoff Brown in the fourth round, although he did win the men's doubles title with his Davis Cup team-mate Frank Parker.

Agassi's room-mate during those London Olympics was a remarkable Iranian heavyweight boxer called Ramak Akabara, a massive circus strong-man with a a perfectly bald head and huge walrus moustache. Akabara, who could pull a car with a tow-rope clenched between his uneven and broken teeth, was a truly fearsome specimen standing 6 feet 8 inches tall. He plied his trade in the Istanbul circus ring where he bent iron bars and wrestled an enormous brown bear.

Ladies of a delicate disposition had been known to swoon and faint as the Persian Colossus inflicted all manner of mayhem upon his body, such as swallowing nails, chewing broken glass, walking over white-hot coals, eating fiery torches and the like. The only trouble was, Akabara was as meek as a lamb in reality and, although he was perfectly happy to endure the most excruciating pain in the furtherance of his profession, was strangely reluctant to inflict the slightest discomfort or suffering upon his fellow man – a small but fatal flaw in a heavyweight fighter. His bouts tended to last only as long as it took his pleasantly surprised opponents to conquer their initial – and quite understandable – trepidation and flatten the benign behemoth with one stroke.

After being thus dealt with in the 1948 Games, the greatly relieved Akabara quit the ring and went on to become one of Europe's most popular circus attractions under his stage name of Ursus the Untameable. Fortunately, unlike his rivals inside the ropes, audiences the world over were completely taken in and this genial giant retired rich and happy to Australia where he had made his home.

Like his reluctant team-mate, Emmanuel Agassi was far from enamoured with boxing and by the time he fought in the 1952 Olympics in Helsinki (no Papp this time, but the middleweight gold medal went to a hard-punching explosive American named Floyd Patterson who would later become the youngest heavyweight champion of all time), tennis had already supplanted the noble art in his heart. During his short time in Finland, he was always far happier practising in the fresh air on the tennis court than he was sparring in the claustrophobic boxing gymnasium, where few were interested in the young Iranian's tales of the top players of the day, Frank Sedgeman, Jaroslav Drobny, Budge Patty and, one of his own personal favourites, Art Larsen.

Apart from being a wonderfully gifted left-hander (rather in the mould of the exquisitely talented Frenchman Henri Leconte), 'Tappy' Larsen was a great eccentric with a vast repertoire of superstitions he had to follow to the absolute letter in the dressing-room before going out on court. His order of dressing was left sock, shirt, left shoe, shorts, right sock, right shoe, touch all four walls, all the while avoiding contact with his reflection in the mirror. His nickname was the result of another curious phenomenon. Larsen claimed he had a recurring nightly dream during which a specific number would become fixed in his mind. Whatever that number, whether one, three, five, nine, seventeen, Larsen would feel compelled to 'tap it out' with his racquet on court the following day. If the number was three he would tap, tap, tap, on the toe of his shoe before he served, tap, tap, tap on the baseline before he received, tap, tap, tap on the umpire's chair every time he changed ends, tap, tap, tap (occasionally) on his opponent's head, and so on.

Larsen, who won the US Championship at Forest Hills in 1950, was sadly forced to give up tennis at the premature

13

age of thirty-two in 1957 after suffering severe head injuries in a motor-cycle accident.

Despite his distaste for the sport, it was his boxing prowess that inspired Emmanuel Agassi in 1952 to bid farewell to his family in Iran for the very last time and set sail for a new life in the United States among the large Armenian community which had settled along the shores of Lake Michigan around Chicago. The nation's second biggest city, which had gained infamy during the years of prohibition from 1919 to 1933, was the industrial heart of America and welcomed immigrant workers who were needed desperately in the iron and steel works, textile and chemical factories, grain mills and meat packing plants.

Not unnaturally, it was to boxing that Agassi first looked for paid employment in his adopted country and after a couple of exhibition bouts he was duly booked to make his professional debut in Madison Square Garden, New York, the 'centre court' of the fight game. The immigrant's attraction for the cynical promoters who were ever on the look-out for a new ethnic 'crowd-pleaser' (i.e. a foreigner who was prone to bleed profusely) owed everything to his freak-value and very little to his questionable prowess. As luck would have it, the inept opponent who had been lined up for Mike 'the Armenian Assassin' Agassi dropped out on doctor's orders with a raging fever shortly before the first bell was due to sound and the Garden's match-maker replaced him with a battle-scarred and ring-wise veteran of over fifty fights renowned for his murderous punching power.

'His record showed he'd had forty or forty-five knockouts in fifty-odd fights,' explains the reluctant pugilist and would-be tennis coach. 'Also, the fight was supposed to be over six rounds and I'd never boxed more than three as an amateur.' Wisely, Mike Agassi took evasive action – he ran. Family folklore suggests he made his apologies to his trainer, rushed to the lavatory, squeezed through a tiny window and proceeded to watch his intended foe bludgeon a bloodied substitute into early retirement on television in a noisy bar on Seventh Avenue. He then caught the first train back to Chicago from Grand Central Station, hurling his boxing gloves out of the window en route. 'And I've never once felt even the slightest temptation to tie them on again.'

Despite his poor English the young ex-prize fighter became a popular figure around his neighbourhood public tennis courts, where a cheerful crowd would quickly form to stare and hurl jovial abuse through the chain-link fence every time he appeared to play. 'I thought he was mad, I truly did,' says Andy Wyglenda, who lived in the same apartment block. 'He was out there in all weathers. Even in January he would shovel snow off the court for four or five hours just so he could play a couple of sets before dark. Up till then I'd always thought tennis was a game for those too delicate to play football or baseball, but Mike was hard as stone. I guess if he'd had the talent to go with the body he'd have won Wimbledon long before his son ever did. I never saw anyone attack a sport with such ferocity.'

After trying his hand at various jobs, Mike Agassi joined an Illinois construction company specialising in up-market homes which came equipped with swimming pools and tennis courts. It was soon obvious to his workmates that he had little or no interest in pursuing a career in pool maintenance or house building. 'My motive was simple, to learn everything there was to know about tennis courts,' recalls Agassi, who soon knew more than his boss and was, predictably, not shy in voicing his opinion. 'One day my boss says to me, "Mike, if I hear one more word from you you're fired." He did and I was.'

The situations vacant columns of the Chicago newspapers of the day proved of no help to the would-be tennis coach, so the ex-construction worker became a trainee waiter at the luxury Ambassador Hotel, and was able to listen in wonderment to the speeches of the two respective Davis Cup captains on the night of 23 August 1959. The flamboyant Perry Jones of the United States spoke of the history and traditions of this great sporting contest, while Harry Hopman, the father of Australian tennis, explained how talent must be nurtured from as young an age as possible. He was the coach who had founded the Australian dynasty which began with the two eighteen-year-old 'boy wonders' Lew Hoad and Ken Rosewall winning the Wimbledon doubles in 1953 and continued through Ashley Cooper, Neale Fraser, Rod Laver, Roy Emerson, Ken Fletcher and Fred Stolle to John Newcombe and Tony Roche.

'It was all so touching that I promised myself I'd have a kid worthy of comparison with all those great Australians, that like Rod Laver and Ken Rosewell the name Agassi would be famous wherever tennis was played. Every parent has a dream for his or her children, that it is their kid who is going to be President of the United States, or the best doctor, the greatest lawyer or the most brilliant scientist. I thought my four were all going to be world champions. Of course, deep down you know it's never going to happen, but it makes it easier to go out on the court day after day and work with the kid in question.'

Following his marriage to Betty and the birth of Rita, Phillip and Tamra (Tami), Mike Agassi had planned to move his family south from Chicago, the windy city, to the tennis friendly climate of California, but a succession of job interviews in Los Angeles led to nothing so instead he opted for another new beginning in Las Vegas. He returned to hotel work while launching himself as a tennis coach to the super-rich visitors who descended upon the neon oasis in the Nevada Desert in the hope of becoming even more super-rich by way of poker, craps, blackjack, baccarat, slot machines or the roulette wheel.

So single-minded was he about his ultimate goal that Betty had to pick out their first home in west Las Vegas without her husband even seeing the interior of the house. While she was checking on what curtains, carpets and gadgets would be needed to make it immediately habitable, Mike was outside measuring the back garden to ensure it would be big enough for a tennis court. He then proceeded to build it with his own hands, at a cost of $21,000, using his months of experience on the Chicago building site as a basis.

This being long before the days when professional tennis coaches could comfortably live off their on-court earnings – like Nick Bollettieri and company – Agassi took a night job at Caesar's Palace, the glitziest hotel and casino complex on Las Vegas Boulevard (better known to all as the Strip), where he quickly climbed the ladder of success and became the showroom captain.

The strange city in which Andre Agassi was born has been dubbed both the gambling and the entertainment capital of the world. Though only 700,000 people actually live in the neat three-storeyed houses which run in rows off the Strip, 22 million visitors a year pour into this strange desert domain with the purpose of either winning $1 million with one intuitive pull on the handle of a one-armed bandit, or seeing people like Frank Sinatra, Barbra Streisand, Dean Martin, Lisa Minelli, George Burns or Joan Rivers performing live in one of the many hotels.

Situated slap-bang in the middle of the desert, Lost Wages, as it is often referred to by the shrewd taxi drivers who work the Strip, was founded in the nineteenth century when a band of settlers wandered off the old Spanish Trail whilst heading for Los Angeles and became lost. A young Mexican scout, Rafael Rivera, was sent out alone to search for water, and after riding across the unexplored sandy waste for 60 miles he happened upon a spring-fed oasis which the Spanish traders who frequently used the route named Las Vegas (the meadows). There was hardly a bush or a tree worth mentioning for 100 miles in any direction and the watering hole was soon a flourishing stop-off point on the map.

In 1885, sixty Mormon settlers sent forth to multiply by Brigham Young set up camp on the outskirts of Las Vegas where they built a stone fortress which stands to this day. They failed in both their attempt to convert the populace to their peculiar way of thinking and the desert into a verdant paradise. Average temperatures of 60°F in the winter and 120°F in the summer might be perfect for budding tennis stars but they are not, particularly the summer temperatures, helpful to budding fruit and vegetables and within eighteen months the Mormons had packed up and headed home to the slightly kinder climes of Salt Lake City.

As the Mormons moved out, the prospectors and grizzled pan handlers moved in to exploit the rich deposits of silver and copper which ran underneath the Nevada and Mojave deserts. By the early 1900s, Rivera's picturesque oasis was an ugly, dusty, tented railroad town of saloons, stores and seedy brothels. When this mini-Klondike ended as suddenly as it had begun, Las Vegas was in danger of becoming just another ghost town populated, as were so many others across what had been the Wild West, only by rattlesnakes, caribou, cacti and the occasional yucca tree.

Two events in 1928, seemingly unrelated, conspired to save the fledgling city: the US Government decided to spend $165 million on building the world's largest antigravity dam at nearby Boulder Canyon, and Governor Fred Balzar signed the bill which legalised gambling in Nevada. He little realised what the final outcome of his handiwork would be.

By 1941 Las Vegas was already a thriving community when New York hotel owner Tommy Hull had a puncture while driving along the Strip. Watching the steady stream of cars heading west to the beaches of California, south to Arizona and east to Colorado, Hull 'got to thinking what a damn fine spot for a hotel I'd stumbled upon' and duly opened El Rancho Vegas, a rooming-house that became infamous for its cheap food and chaotic poker tables. The success of Hull's new venture did not pass unnoticed in New York and Chicago, where the Mafia was always on the lookout for 'legal' ways of laundering their ill-gotten gains. With the financial assistance of Lucky Luciano and Meyer Lansky, Benjamin 'Bugsy' Siegal (head of the mob's numerous operations on the West Coast) opened the Fabulous Flamingo, a shocking-pink concrete wedding cake of a building set amid an oasis of palm trees. The legendary Jimmy Durante appeared as Master of Ceremonies on opening night, 26 December 1946.

But Siegal had fatally miscalculated. Though the 'joint was jumpin'' every night, the Fabulous Flamingo mysteriously operated at a loss. Six months later the boys in New York ran out of patience – and Bugsy out of time. His subsequent gangland slaying, which Mario Puzo immortalised in *The Godfather* when he describes the Corleone family's 'removal' of Moe Green, a character based on the luckless Bugsy, was headline news across the nation. As rumours of mob involvement intensified, thrill seekers flocked to Las Vegas to rub shoulders with the heavies and the Hollywood celebrities who attended them.

Using the Strip as its private Monopoly board, the Mafia built hotels everywhere, the Riviera, the Dunes, the Sands (where Sinatra regularly topped the bill with the Count Basie Orchestra), the Sahara, the Stardust. Outraged by this blatant take-over, the US Government belatedly took action and hurriedly passed a law making it illegal for known criminals or their associates to become partners, sleeping or otherwise, in hotels and casinos.

By the mid-1960s Las Vegas was in dire peril for the second time in its brief but colourful history, and luck again conspired to save it. An unlikely saviour rode quietly into town one evening hidden away behind the blacked-out windows of his private luxury train. Howard Hughes, multi-millionaire and eccentric recluse, aviator, film producer and entrepreneur, had just sold Trans-World Airlines for $550 million and was looking for something new to divert his attention, so he snapped up a chain of four hotels, the local television station and McCarran International Airport.

According to the legend, Hughes only became interested in the casino business when he arrived incognito at the Desert

Inn Hotel and was brusquely informed there were no rooms available that night due to the number of high rollers in town. Hughes simply bought the entire hotel on the spot. Whatever the reasons, the arrival of a genuine all-American hero undoubtedly 'legitimised' gambling in the eyes of many, and today, not only is every major chain represented, but the ten biggest hotels in the world are all to be found in Las Vegas, including the 5,000-room MGM Grand, the 4,000-room Excalibur, and the 3,000-room Mirage, owned by Andre Agassi's long-time close friend, Steve Wynn.

The Excalibur, a fantasy land castle of red, white and blue turrets, is best described as Blackpool-on-Speed and comes equipped with a 100,000-square-foot casino, the Lance-a-Lotta pizzeria, 'Ye Olde Village Fayre' with roll-a-penny stalls, darts and coconut shies, plus the horses, armour and handsome jousting knights of King Arthur's Tournament (held twice nightly in the Wembley Stadium-sized basement).

Though it is Caesar's Palace which remains the playground of the serious gambler (world poker champion Amarillo Slim Preston, Telly Savalas and Timothy '007' Dalton are among those who immediately head there when in Las Vegas on business), the Mirage, a 'South Seas Paradise' built by Wynn for a figure well in excess of $630 million, currently stands unrivalled as the biggest attraction around. At night, the incessant traffic along the three-and-a-half miles of the Strip slows to a crawl as the roaring waterfalls in the curved driveway regularly erupt into a disturbingly realistic fiery volcano.

Incidentally, Wynn also owns the Golden Nugget Hotel and Casino in downtown Las Vegas, an eye-catching marble edifice boasting gold-plated elevators, telephone booths and slot-machines, and the 'world's largest gold nugget', a 63-pound chunk of yellow rock valued at over $1 million, which was mined in Australia but now stands behind a plate-glass window in the hotel lobby.

But the homecoming 1992 Wimbledon champion staged his

celebration party at the Mirage. The guests danced to the strains of a samba band under the vast glass-domed atrium which houses a verdant Amazonian rain forest. The vegetation is the real thing, and the intermittent showers are provided by a computerised sprinkler system. 'It's the neatest place I've ever been,' says Agassi, who has been to Paris, Rome, Sydney, Prague, Barcelona, New Orleans . . .

In this world of make-believe, the two most important individuals – certainly as far as the millions of visitors are concerned – are the pit bosses, who run the casinos and therefore decide which big-spending guests are eligible for free hotel rooms, meals and cabaret tickets, and the show-room captains, whose job it is to find a seat for those lucky enough to have secured precious passes for the Diana Ross Show or suchlike.

Thus not only did Mike Agassi come to see and hear all the star names of show business – Sinatra, Ann-Margret, Sammy Davis Jr, Billy Eckstine, Tony Bennett, George Burns, Nat King Cole, Jerry Lewis – but he received financial bonanzas in the form of generous tips from those grateful and treasured clients rewarded with a prime table. A crisp $100 bill is usually sufficient in Las Vegas to secure a prized booth complete with luxurious padded leather upholstery within touching distance of Frank, Lisa or Engelbert; a tatty ten-spot, however, will be 'rewarded' with a hopeless seat at an out-of-the-way table hidden behind a pillar where you are likely to crick your neck craning to catch even the merest glimpse of your favourite star on the stage above.

As a favoured employee, first at Caesar's Palace, then across Las Vegas Boulevard at Bally's Casino Resort, Mike Agassi was on first-name terms with all the top-of-the-bill entertainers, the great boxers who fought there – Muhammad Ali, Joe Frazier, Larry Holmes, Sugar Ray Leonard and George Foreman among them – plus the regular flow of tennis players who stayed at the various five-star complexes after playing exhibition matches.

The superb 14,000-capacity show court in the back garden of Caesar's, where a huge marble statue of Apollo stands guard over the toga-clad cocktail goddesses, has witnessed any number of intriguing tennis clashes over the years. It was here in 1975 that the brash young Jimmy Connors thrashed Rod Laver in the much-hyped Battle of the Generations, and here that forty-year-old Connors would beat Martina Navratilova in the Battle of the Sexes III in September 1992. Andre Agassi, who could scarcely see over the net, traded blows with his childhood hero Bjorn Borg during an interval in the Alan King Classic on the same court.

Having taught himself to string that very first tattered old racquet back in Tehran, Mike Agassi, as well as giving coaching lessons, also opened a restringing business which very quickly became the most successful in the whole of Nevada and a regular haunt for the leading players of the day. By the time Andre Agassi, who was born on 29 April 1970, was a precocious four-year-old, he had already 'knocked-up' with Connors, Borg and Pancho Gonzales, his brother-in-law-to-be. 'When he beats me,' said Connors, pointing at the tiny tot, 'I'll know it's time to retire.' The old warrior has since been beaten many times but is still waiting to make good that promise.

Although all four Agassi siblings spent many long hours every day on the tennis court in the family back yard as their father put them through a rigorous practice schedule under the unforgiving desert sun, there was but one potential Wimbledon champion among the flock. Rita possessed the talent but not the single-mindedness, Tami had the determination but not the natural prowess, while Phil was neither good nor committed enough to carve out a full-time career as a professional.

'They were all good, really good, but Andre was always that little bit better,' says Mike, who had suspended a tennis ball on a string over Andre's crib when he was only a few days old and first put a cut-down racquet in his tiny hand when he was but a week old. 'In fact he was a little bit different from any of the kids who came to me for lessons. He had these huge eyes, and I mean really, really huge eyes.

'Even as a tiny baby he was able to follow the flight of a ball through the air. I first noticed that when I spotted him doing it at a table tennis tournament in the Frontier Hotel. That's a gift he was born with, no kid in the world can be taught to do that. Eventually he reached out to touch, first with his hand, then with one of his mother's serving spoons. Always he makes contact. I tell you, wherever the ball is, there is Andre . . . just waiting. After a few months I tied a balloon to his high chair when he was having his meals, and pretty soon he was lashing out at it with a tiny table tennis paddle.

'As soon as he could walk he started hitting a ball against the wall of his bedroom and he'd only ever go to sleep at night if his racquet was tucked up in bed beside him. By the age of two – and remember he was small for his age – Andre was already serving overhead into a full court. When people say it was me who taught him to play I say "no". Andre was born with a racquet in his hand. He was born to play tennis. He was born to be a great champion. I gave him only the mechanics, the desire, the will to win.'

Andre was no sooner toddling around the couple's five-bedroomed home in west Las Vegas than his father handed him a full-sized adult racquet which he would use to launch cups, saucers and glasses into orbit. The local glazier was a regular visitor, constantly being called upon to repair the windows broken by the flying crockery.

It was around age six that Agassi, who also loved to ride his bicycle as fast as possible, began to develop the style of play which remains the hallmark of his game today. 'I explained to him that the earlier he hits the ball the better, as soon as possible after it has bounced and while it is still rising. That's how come he can hit it back so hard. I also taught him to angle his returns, the sharpest angle he dared. I say to him, "Do this right and the other guy has to call a cab to get to the ball,"' explains Mike.

23

Agassi senior may not have enjoyed any formal tennis teaching as such, but he read every book about the subject he could lay his hands on, rented films and visited factories all over Nevada and California to discover how balls and racquets were manufactured. 'Dad slept a maximum of six hours a night for I don't know how many years,' remembers Rita. 'He had no real life of his own during all that time.'

He came to believe that his sheer hard work more than compensated for his own lack of specialised training. 'It's easy to get people's money by telling them to bend their knees and take the racquet head back. There are twelve or fifteen basic tips which all the pros know, but there was nobody around back then who could teach you how to hit the ball at 125 mph or with no pace at all.' A firm advocate of 'practice makes perfect' – 'I feel that hitting 4,000 balls in two hours is better than 2,000 balls in four hours' – Mike Agassi's personal theories still cause raised eyebrows to this day among those of a more traditional outlook.

The court on which Andre Agassi learned to play tennis resembled a junkyard. Thirty-six dustbins full of balls were arrayed along the sidelines and three ball machines pumped out an incessant barrage of 110 mph serves. 'There's no human opponent I know of who can provide 600 or 700 successive serves bang on the line,' explains Mike, whose machines can also deliver topspin, backspin and slice, forehands, backhands and volleys, drop shots, lobs and angled returns. 'I guess that between the age of three and thirteen Andre must have hit well over a million balls a year. Like Harry Hopman, I really believed that if a kid started early enough and had the proper training and coaching you could make him or her a world champion. All you really need to succeed at tennis is fast eye–hand co-ordination.'

By tinkering with the thirteen different ball machines in his back yard, Mike Agassi put together a serving device which he placed just above the net and could fire 100 mph bullet 'serves' into the far corners of the service box. 'That's how Andre learned to return serve, and that's why it's still the best part of his game, as everyone saw at Wimbledon.'

Though many coaches will disagree, the amateur tennis professor insists his adopted sport is more of a wrist game than an arm game. 'No matter what anyone else said, I knew that's where the power lay. In boxing, a short, sharp hook is far more powerful than a straight left because it is generated with the wrist. Even a handkerchief thrown at you at 180 mph will simply float to the ground, but if I hold it and flick it at you with a snap of my wrist, that handkerchief can make your nose bleed.'

Mary Rowan, the daughter of the family's original neighbours in Las Vegas, trained under Mike Agassi for seven years: 'He was the first coach I ever came across who made you hit every ball as hard as you could. At some point, he reasoned, you would learn to control it. Sure he expected 100 per cent, but all this talk of him being some kind of an ogre is bull. He demanded you do your very best, but that was all he ever asked. Every lesson was free because (a) he loved tennis, and (b) he loved children. He was a very warm and gentle man, so I have to laugh whenever I read how he "drove" Andre. No way. It was Andre who had to be physically dragged off court every day.'

Mike Agassi has similar memories: 'Behind all the great kids – Courier, Chang, Seles – are parents who gave everything they could. Parents who don't resent spending everything they can afford and who didn't mind standing behind them all those years. Never mind what I wanted, Andre could never have been a world champion if he hadn't desired it so much. I remember he used to invent games just so he could stay out there on the court a little while longer. He'd put a couple of balls in his pocket and four in his hand and say, "Connors forehand," "Nastase backhand," "Laver volley" and hit a perfect replica of the called shot.'

As Borg, Connors and Courier had, Agassi took up tennis

at such a tender age he was scarcely able to hold his sawn-off racquet in one hand, which is why he first developed the two-fisted backhand that was to become a trademark as immediately recognisable as his bleached blond locks and graffiti-splattered ensembles.

Stanford Stevens III, who chose to study American history rather than develop his own promising tennis prowess, remembers playing the future Wimbledon champion in the first round of an under-tens junior tournament at Newport Beach, California, in the late autumn of 1977, and recalls that meeting as 'like being run over by an out-of-control four-foot juggernaut'. 'I was pretty good for my age, or so I'd thought up till that day, but Andre was something else again. Even then you could sort of sense he was a one-off. He walloped every ball as though he never wanted to see it again – and invariably he didn't because most of his shots were impossible to return. It was hard work just staying in the rally with him, let alone actually winning a point. At that stage I'd have to say he was virtually unbeatable.

'For his age and tiny size he had this tremendous serve and he had no inhibitions about giving the ball a mighty whack on both his forehand and backhand. I also seem to remember that he would charge up to the net at almost every opportunity, which was something none of us kids from California did, even though he could hardly see over the top of it back then. We were all locked into Connors and Evert at that time and it would never have crossed our minds to venture away from the baseline. We only ever came to the net to shake hands with our opponent at the end of the match. Andre cleaned me out 6–0, 6–0, the first time I'd ever been beaten zip-and-zip. Still, it's not everyone who gets to lose to the champion of Wimbledon, is it?'

Though Mike Agassi was holding down two jobs, while Betty worked full-time for the State of Nevada Department of Employment, life was a constant financial struggle for the family. Las Vegas may have offered the perfect climate in which to hone their children's tennis skills, but the nearest important tournaments were all staged in southern California, a full ten hours' drive away, and every weekend had to be carefully arranged with the precision of a military operation. Each Friday night while Mike was busily engaged at Bally's Casino (he would later drive like crazy through the dark to catch up with his family), Betty would load up the family estate car with four children, six suitcases, twenty racquets and a motley assortment of tennis shoes, sweatbands and socks.

Tennis in California was, and remains so even in these supposedly more liberal 1990s, very much the private preserve of the wealthy classes, so this red-eyed Iranian immigrant, all belligerent resentment, and his dishevelled troupe were a constant source of irritation at the genteel country clubs, inspiring a whispered torrent of snobbish smirks and snide comments. 'Yes, looking back now I think it is definitely fair to say we were discriminated against,' admits Mike. 'They didn't like the way we looked or the way the kids played.'

Nor did the suntanned attorneys, dentists and bankers of southern California and their pampered progeny relish the manner in which the Agassis, father and children alike, behaved on or off the tennis court. Indeed, Mike Agassi was the subject of countless letters of complaint because of his language (though Armenian was his first language it was said he could curse his offspring in English for a full twenty minutes without using the same swearword twice) and his intimidating behaviour towards officials and fellow-parents. At any match involving any of the Agassis, sporting handshakes were all but unknown (however, fisticuffs were not) and it was not uncommon for Mike Agassi to be very politely asked to remove himself from the premises post-haste.

On one occasion he was even barred from continuing to attend a tournament after a complaint from a thirteen-year-old girl that he had verbally abused her. Another day, another tournament and another match, this time involving Tami. Weary of hearing Mike applaud his daughter's frequent errors, the rival father

27

asked him to desist, whereupon, according to onlookers, Agassi senior 'went absolutely ape' and explained in graphic detail how he had broken the legs of the last person to argue with him.

'There's no doubt Mike Agassi had a serious problem in dealing with his own children, let alone anyone from outside the family group,' recalls another professional tennis coach working in Las Vegas around the same time. 'He was always looking for a reason to fight, always complaining about something, the draw was rigged or the kids had been given an unfavourable court. And it was common knowledge he threatened everyone who crossed him. It was no surprise the kids were badly behaved, too. They weren't bad in the sense they were wicked or anything. They'd just become accustomed to seeing their father try to bend the rules on their behalf, like illegally offering coaching instructions during matches. Their language also raised a few eyebrows. Actually it would have raised a few eyebrows among the GIs in an army canteen, never mind among the members of a sedate tennis club.

'Mike was really caught up with Andre becoming number one: number one in the county, then number one in the state, then number one in the under-twelves, then number one in the under-fifteens – and ultimately number one in the world.'

While the four Agassi siblings ranted and raved on court, their pugnacious father was wont to rail against anyone or anything he perceived as being unhelpful or unsympathetic to the family's cause: 'At the time it did seem to me like we were always being asked to play first thing at seven thirty or eight o'clock in the morning. Is that fair after driving over the desert all night? When I complained, they'd snap back: "Well no one asked you to bring your kids here." When you're broke, working every hour every day, trying to save every dime, your temper tends to be on a short fuse. That is not an excuse, but an explanation maybe for why certain things happened.

'But people on the outside probably don't realise that the majority of tennis parents tend to be phoneys. They can't see anybody better than their own kid. Not me. In fact I always liked to see someone beat Andre occasionally, just to see how they did it and how he accepted it.' Unsurprisingly, Rita also views those early days somewhat differently from the Agassi family's hostile band of critics: 'There's no doubt in my mind that many of the other parents were resentful just because my dad's methods worked. And he'd help anyone he could, he really would, and not just his own children. The Armenians have this real strong sense of family. And if you're the head of it, then you have to protect your family and do what you believe is right for them. My dad has lived his whole life protecting us and doing what he believes is right. I guess the other families were plain jealous . . .

'And despite what everyone thought, Dad knew what he was doing. He truly is an incredible guy when you get to know him. He has this amazing amount of knowledge about all sorts of different subjects. He's so innovative that I've no doubt he could have done anything he set out to do. If he'd wanted to raise an entire family of kids who all graduated from college by the age of fourteen, I honestly believe he could have done just that.'

Mike Agassi left Bally's Casino three years ago to design racquets for Donnay. He still gives free coaching lessons in Las Vegas, though he admits: 'As far as that side of tennis is concerned, I guess my life's work was done when Andre became Wimbledon champion.'

When not playing tennis, Andre was like any normal seven-year-old; he detested school, where his attention span was minimal – 'like that of a goldfish' wrote one teacher on his annual report card – he liked swimming, skate-boarding, and, much to his surprise, the pretty dark-haired girl next door.

By the time she was five, Wendy Stewart had a mad crush on Andre, and while he was out belting tennis balls for hours at a time against the back wall of his wooden bungalow, she was happily acting as dedicated ball girl. 'Ever since they were toddlers, Wendy and Andre were always in and out of one another's houses,' explains her father, Manny Stewart. 'They were inseparable, and unlike most kids of that age they never once fell out. I don't remember any tears, bloodied noses or anything like that.

'Wendy always idolised Andre, still does. I guess she would have run to the ends of the earth if he'd asked her. You seldom saw Andre any place without a tennis racquet in his hand. Even if he was just strolling down the sidewalk, you could be certain he'd be trailing a racquet behind him. During the school vacation he'd spend all day out in that dusty back yard of his while Wendy followed him around like a faithful little puppy throwing tennis balls for him to hit. When it finally became too hot for even Andre to stay outside, they would come indoors and sit holding hands together on the sofa watching the cartoons on television with an ice-cold soda and cookies.'

Despite Wendy's calming influence Andre grew ever more frustrated at the perceived injustices meted out by the tennis establishment, at the 1,200-mile round trips he had to make to California just to find a reasonably worthy opponent, and at the amount of time he was 'wasting by attending school when there's nothing more I need learn'. 'There's only two ways to go in Las Vegas when you're a teenager,' he explains reflectively, 'good or bad. There's no middle road. I suppose I was only twelve or so but I could tell I was falling into a deep hole. I was gradually becoming the type of person who'd drink, yeah, even as a twelve-year-old, become a loudmouth and get into trouble of some kind. There was a gang of us guys and we'd go to a drive-in movie and sit around getting drunk and causing mischief.'

An insular child whose only real contact with other boys was as a deadly rival across a tennis net, Agassi can readily admit now that, 'I distanced myself from people as I got older. It was my own choice. Looking back, I guess that teenage gang was the closest thing to a social life I ever had in Vegas. I can only remember having one real, close friend.'

Of all the cities in the United States, Las Vegas is perhaps the last place in which one would choose to grow up.

When one flies into Las Vegas's McCarran International Airport, it is always a shock to the eye when, amidst a seemingly never-ending scorched moonscape of mountains, rock formations, sand and giant cacti, the modern metropolis of concrete and neon suddenly looms into view shimmering through the desert heat-haze. Though you can gamble 24 hours a day, 365 days a year here, it is a city that only really comes to life after darkness falls. The 3½-mile-long Strip is ablaze with fabulous illuminations, like the 183-foot multi-coloured sign outside the Stardust Casino, which is visible from far out in the desert, and the 222-foot electronic billboard proclaiming the whereabouts of the Sahara Hotel.

Only in Las Vegas can visitors don a swimsuit and play blackjack at a table floating in the middle of the Hacienda Hotel's indoor pool, clamber aboard a full-size carousel complete with revolving horses and feed dollar coins into a rotating slot-machine, or stand at a roulette wheel while a live circus of clowns, trapeze artists, jugglers and high-wire walkers perform on the glass floor overhead.

Only in Las Vegas will you find beautiful cocktail waitresses dressed as harem dancers, Polynesian maidens, Roman slave girls, medieval damsels and Wild West saloon singers in outfits guaranteed accurate down to the last detail, the world's largest casino floor (bigger even than two football pitches laid side-by-side), the world's largest and most vulgar gift shop, the world's largest video store (the horror movies are kept in a room shaped like a coffin, the musicals in a huge walk-in yellow submarine), a church where all donations are made in casino chips (once a week the priest lugs the offering down to Caesar's Palace to be turned into cash), and a 24-hour wedding chapel (where Bruce Willis, Joan Collins and Bette Midler have all paid $75 to be married at three o'clock in the morning).

Those who wish to abandon the one-armed bandits, however

briefly, and head off in search of culture can visit the Liberace Museum, where the pianist's faithful sister-in-law Dora Liberace presides over a kitsch collection of his pianos (one was owned by Chopin, another by George Gershwin), his assorted stage outfits (including one outrageous little number styled after the coronation robes of King George V), and where you can buy a commemorative Liberace ashtray, toilet roll holder, wig, musical lavatory seat, or life-sized inflatable doll.

It is still possible to hear the music of the great man himself, or at least a passably accurate impersonation, at Legends in Concert, a kind of high-class karaoke night at the Imperial Palace Hotel (a vast peacock-blue pagoda) where a cast of professional lookalikes and soundalikes offer their renditions of the greatest hits of Roy Orbison, Buddy Holly, Judy Garland and Louis Armstrong. An emotion-charged climax features the 'ever-popular' (according to the glaring neon billboard at least) Elvis Presley impersonator Tony Roy in white rhinestone jumpsuit belting out 'Viva Las Vegas'.

Those who prefer a 'live' show can choose from any one of twenty, the hottest ticket in town currently being that of Siegfried and Roy's 'Beyond Belief' act at the Mirage where Steve Wynn is paying the two spellbinding illusionists $55.5 million over five years to make elephants, lions, tigers and Chevrolets disappear nightly into thin air. Across the way at the Jubilee Nightclub, a cast of a hundred – with the not inconsiderable aid of some stupendous, eye-popping special effects – recreates the sinking of the *Titanic* and other such misadventures while a chorus of showgirls sashay around in fabulous head-dresses (and very little else) costing $5,000 and weighing 40 pounds each, all created by Hollywood designer Bob Mackie, the man responsible for many of rock singer Cher's most outlandish creations.

There are other oddities. In a throwback to the early days, some hotels still refuse to provide television sets in the rooms, thereby 'encouraging' guests to spend even more of their time and money in the casino; and swimming pools, in a city which boasts 315 sunny days a year, tend to close at around 5 p.m. for precisely the same mercenary reason. While all drinks are free on the casino floor, the gullible quickly discover that this is merely just another ruse to loosen any surviving inhibitions gamblers might otherwise feel about squandering their hard-earned dollars on the turn of a card or the throw of a dice.

Here then is the atmosphere in which Andre Agassi spent his formative years, a world of fantasy and fraud, of glamour and glitz, of show business and spectacle; a world built by the Mafia and visited by the greedy, a world in which parents can deposit their offspring in a hostel where they will be fed, watered and looked after for an entire weekend while Mom and Pop devote their entire attention to the spinning roulette wheel. It has been said, with justification, that when Las Vegas was built it spoiled a nice desert.

The only time Agassi was given a genuine test of his precocious abilities was when his eldest sister Rita, who now runs her brother's official fan club from her home in Las Vegas, and her husband dropped by.

Pancho Gonzales is remembered mainly as the greatest player never to have won the Wimbledon men's singles championship, though Ken Rosewall and Ilie Nastase also have strong claims to this unfortunate title. Nevertheless, for most of the 1950s he was undisputedly the best player in the world, king of the touring professional circus which included such all-time greats as Jack Kramer, Budge Patty, Frank Sedgeman and Tony Trabert. If tennis had gone 'open' in the summer of 1960, as it so very nearly did, Gonzales, then aged thirty-two, might just have edged out Lew Hoad, Ken Rosewall and Alex Olmedo to win the Wimbledon title denied him for a decade. But by the time tennis did open its doors to the great stars of the professional circuit eight years later, Gonzales was a venerable forty. He was still good enough to be seeded eighth, behind

Rod Laver, Ken Rosewall, Andres Gimeno, John Newcombe, Roy Emerson, Manuel Santana and Lew Hoad, but no longer a genuine contender for the trophy he coveted above all others.

True, he survived two rounds against that elegant player Ramanathan Krishnan, father of India's current number one, Ramesh, and Australian Bob Maud at that first 'open' Wimbledon, but Gonzales was not at ease on the fast grass and went out in four sets in the third round to the emerging Alex Metreveli from Soviet Georgia, who would be a popular runner-up to Jan Kodes in the 1973 final. Twelve months later, at forty-one, Gonzales would contest what romantics still believe to be the most exciting Centre Court match of all time when he met fellow-American Charlie Pasarell, almost twenty years his junior, in the first round.

Pasarell, who now serves on the board of directors of the Association of Tennis Professionals (ATP), was something of a Wimbledon specialist, having beaten Santana in 1967 on the only occasion on which the defending champion has been dethroned in the first round, and having narrowly lost to Rosewall in five sets the following year. On Tuesday 23 June 1969, he walked out on the Centre Court for the third successive year at the All England Club, this time to face his boyhood idol and one-time private coach.

The match, which began in the deepening gloom of a murky summer's evening, finally ended on the Wednesday afternoon after a total of five hours and twenty minutes' play and with Gonzales, who was a firm believer in Groucho Marx's famous assertion that 'a man is only as old as the woman he feels', the unlikely victor by the astonishing scoreline of 22–24, 1–6, 16–14, 6–3, 11–9. Though nineteen games more than Wimbledon's previous longest encounter, Jaroslav Drobny's epic third-round victory over Budge Patty in 1953, the figures alone cannot convey the nerve jangling emotion of the occasion.

The greying Gonzales, already a senior citizen in tennis

terms, did not enjoy the assistance of such recent innovations as the tie-break or even a canvas chair on which to rest his weary limbs during the many change-overs; his face haunted and drawn, he certainly looked a beaten man after losing a titanic tussle for the first set during which his younger opponent ruthlessly wore him down by hoisting a succession of strength sapping lobs. A full two decades after winning the Wimbledon doubles title, Gonzales was experiencing extreme difficulty in picking out the ball against the increasingly dark background and Pasarell began the second set in merciless mood with a series of thumping service winners.

An understandably grumpy Gonzales had repeatedly asked umpire Harold Duncombe, an elderly gentleman of school-masterly aspect in trilby hat and raincoat, this being the days before professional umpires, to abandon the match because of the failing light. Three times the American beseeched Duncombe to summon referee Captain Mike Gibson and three times the stern-faced official declined to do so. Pasarell moved inexorably ahead under cover of darkness. There can be no question Gonzales threw away the second set 6–1, and when Gibson finally called a halt to the farce, the veteran American skulked off the Centre Court to a chorus of boos after assaulting the umpire's chair with his racquet. He muttered, he swore, he gesticulated and few of the spectators there that night doubted Gonzales had accepted defeat in his own heart and mind.

When play resumed the following afternoon it seemed inevitable that Pasarell would win, for although Gonzales managed to stay level throughout the third set, the older man was coming under increasing mental and physical pressure. But at 8–8 and 10–10 Pasarell fatally squandered two gilt-edged opportunities to break serve and the match began to swing imperceptibly but dramatically away from him. Gonzales, who had regularly taught his opponent and therefore knew his game inside out, pounced at 15–14 with the aid of two double faults, a recurrent flaw in Pasarell's game which would stop him ever reaching the very top echelon of the game as a singles player.

Though Gonzales was visibly exhausted, he continued to cover the court with the grace and guile of a big cat and levelled the match at two sets apiece when he captured Pasarell's once-dominant serve in the seventh game of the fourth set with a breathtaking lob which landed on the line as gently as a snowflake.

The longer the fifth set went on, however, the hopes of the Centre Court crowd, who had by then taken the middle-aged magician to their hearts, grew ever fainter and the end seemed nigh when Gonzales put three weary volleys into the foot of the net to trail 4–5, 0–40. Three match points. Two Pasarell lobs, both of which overshot the baseline by millimetres, and a searing ace staved off the danger on that occasion, though Gonzales managed to level at 5–5 only after seven nail biting deuces. At 5–6, the old champion was in trouble again as Pasarell gained another three match points at 0–40. With the tension almost too much to bear, Gonzales again squirmed to safety with a service winner and a brace of outrageous yet delicate stop volleys.

Those two shots comprise arguably the greatest successive points ever witnessed on the Centre Court. They would have been regarded as minor miracles in a practice session, but, from a 41-year-old player on the edge of physical and mental exhaustion at match point down in the fifth set at Wimbledon, who had to lean on his racquet between points and who could scarcely move because of cramp in his legs, they were sheer witchcraft.

But still Gonzales was not out of the fire. At 7–8 Pasarell again reached 30–40 – match point number seven – and again victory was denied him when another beautifully disguised lob cleared the very tip of Gonzales' desperately outstretched racquet, only to drift agonisingly over the baseline. If it had been a boxing match, Captain Gibson would have stopped the fight to save Gonzales further punishment. He had given his all and then some, and could no longer offer even token resistance. Though he could still stand upright to serve, Gonzales was spent. To all intents and purposes he was completely immobilised.

Then from 9–10, 15–15, Gonzales was suddenly a dashing 21-year-old again as he reeled off eleven points in succession with blistering aces, flashing forehands, delicate backhands, acrobatic smashes and stunning volleys. Too old to be a champion, Wimbledon had a new sporting god. It was always an impossible dream, of course, but Gonzales went on to defeat both Sweden's Ove Bengtson and fellow-American Tom Edlefsen in straight sets before narrowly losing to the fifth-seeded Arthur Ashe in the fourth round.

This was the larger-than-life super-hero who incurred the not inconsiderable wrath of Mike Agassi when he married Rita, thirty-five years his junior. Even though Pancho and Rita Gonzales have since separated, the great champion followed his young ex-brother-in-law's every match at Wimbledon on television from his home in Las Vegas, and, two months later, was a constant and vociferous courtside presence at the 1992 US Open at Flushing Meadow where Agassi reached the quarter-finals before going down to his old adversary Courier.

Ten years ago, however, Gonzales was seldom made to feel entirely comfortable in the Agassi household, where the first fissures between father and teenage son were just beginning to appear. Andre had by now left the First Good Shepherd junior school in Las Vegas and was about to attend Cashman High with his boyhood pal Perry Rogers, a friendship formed during an under-eleven tournament and which survives to this day. Back in 1982, Agassi and Rogers were inseparable, whether it was going to a movie house, playing tennis, soccer, one-on-one basketball, hookey, swimming or raising up a dust storm on the streets of Las Vegas.

'They weren't bad, just a bit wild,' recalls Jackie Jovanovic, who had been a classmate at the First Good Shepherd for a term. 'It was common knowledge they drank beer and hung around with a bunch of older guys outside school, but there was never any question of violence or bullying. I think everyone just viewed Andre as a spoiled brat because of the way his father treated him.'

But no sooner had he started classes at Cashman High than it was time for father and son ('Have you met my little world champ?' is how Mike Agassi liked to introduce the four-year-old Andre) to sever their claustrophobic relationship. Though he had heard reports of the place, Agassi senior had little knowledge of the Nick Bollettieri Tennis Academy until he saw a television programme dedicated to the camp that included grim scenes of sobbing thirteen-year-olds being put through a gruelling routine of parade ground drills. Despite the prohibitive tuition fees, a whopping $2,300 per month, Mike Agassi immediately decided here was the ideal 'school' for his wayward, if richly talented, offspring, who was already the undisputed under-fifteen racquet and tantrum throwing champion of all Nevada.

He sought the various opinions of other coaches, an unusual occurrence in itself, and everyone agreed his son would fare better in Bradenton where he would have to face the very best players in his age group from all over the world, plus the academy's notorious marine corps discipline. For once, even Andre was in full agreement with his father. 'Sure I wanted to go, why not? Actually I really didn't feel there was much of a choice at the time as I wasn't exactly the kind to stay at school or become a college kid. I don't know what I'd have done if I'd had to work for eight hours in an office, or anywhere else but on a tennis court, so it was my own decision as much as Dad's.'

Gonzales, who had studied the boy from an early age, muses: 'If he'd stayed in Vegas he'd have been one heck of a tennis player . . . but only by sending him away to Bollettieri or to another top coach was Mike going to turn him into a world champion.'

3

Alcatraz-on-Sea

The night before he was to leave his Las Vegas home for the Nick Bollettieri Tennis Academy in Florida, Andre Agassi, accompanied as ever by Perry Rogers, hired a chauffeur-driven stretch-limousine and drifted around his favourite haunts until what Sinatra would crooningly describe as 'the wee small hours of the morning'. With $100 in their collective back pocket, a benefaction from a possibly guilt-ridden father, the two thirteen-year-olds dined out on southern fried chicken fingers at Tramps, burgers and French fries at Binion's, strawberry milk shakes at Mary's Diner and double chocolate chip ice-creams at Ralph's Place. As they drove they ate, and as they ate they talked over 'old' times while cruising up and down their beloved neonlit Strip.

For all his brazen cockiness, Agassi was little different from any other adolescent of such an age; underneath the defiant bubble gum chewing, the swaggering, belligerent confidence, he was, as Rogers knew, secretly in dread of leaving Las Vegas, of leaving his comfortable home life, his family and friends, the security of all his familiar surroundings.

Though he remembers feeling like 'a condemned man enjoying one last night of freedom', Agassi has also been quoted as saying: 'I guess I had to get away from my dad. But please don't take that the wrong way. I really loved him, I still do. But looking back to that time I guess I was the type of person who could easily have destroyed my relationship with my mother or father if I felt they weren't being fair.' Certainly, there can be little doubt that as far as their on-court tennis playing relationship was concerned, father and son had gone just about as far as they could go. If Andre had remained at home in Las Vegas much beyond his thirteenth birthday, he would have grown increasingly sullen and rebellious and, in all probability, thrown away his sneakers and been lost to the sport for all time.

But despite his many and varied misgivings, if Agassi was expecting Alcatraz-on-Sea as he drove along the Gulf of Mexico coast through the beach resorts of Tampa and Palmetto to Bradenton the following afternoon, he was pleasantly surprised by the scene which met his eyes when he swept up the driveway of 5500 West 34th Street. Bollettieri's supposed jailhouse turned out to resemble a Butlin's holiday camp sugar-coated in flamingo-pink icing; the palm trees swayed gently in the balmy ocean breezes, the rays of the brilliant Florida sun danced on the inviting pool, and a cluster of confident teenage girls with perfect *café au lait* tans and legs the length of the Champs Elysées strolled by in designer tennis gear.

A friendly 'red coat' showed Bollettieri's latest guest around the impressive 25-acre complex, which houses seventy-five all-weather, floodlit courts (four indoor for the considerately rare shower of Florida rain), gymnasium, aerobic centre, sports science laboratory, research department, cinema, canteen, games room and library, before leaving him to unpack his belongings in his new home, the two-bedroomed cottage he was to share with seven other fellow students. One of whom was to be Jim Courier, a thoughtful fourteen-year-old flame-haired innocent only newly-arrived himself from Dade City, Florida.

Those first impressions were misleading, however, for this was no Butlin's holiday camp, despite the heady mix of sun, sea and lissom brown bodies. In his teenage excitement and relief, the young apprentice had failed to spot the two uniformed security guards with slavering German Shepherds manning the front gates; the aquamarine pool, he soon discovered, was for the use of visiting parents only and strictly out of bounds to their sweaty offspring, and there, waiting to greet him with a perfect (and perfectly rehearsed) toothy smile, was a discipline-crazy ex-paratrooper with a detestation of insubordination.

Nick Bollettieri could only happen in America. If you were to believe everything they say about this suntanned Svengali, you would gradually concoct an alarming identikit picture portraying the ruthless ambition of Macbeth, the mysticism of Rasputin, the persuasive powers of Billy Graham and the dress sense of Coco the Clown.

He has been variously described as 'undoubtedly one of the world's best tennis coaches' (*Wall Street Journal*), 'a con job. He knows nothing about tennis' (John McEnroe), 'a terrible man who produces robots' (*Spectator*), 'the Merchant of Tennis' (*Daily News*), 'the game's Michelangelo of the eighties' (Nick Bollettieri) and 'Nick Bollettieri is to beautiful tennis what Hannibal Lecter is to vegetarian cooking' (anonymous).

'You can't be too concerned about what people say about you,' intones Bollettieri, whose business card is embossed: 'Tennis instructor, coach and motivator'. 'If you try to fight all the negative publicity which flies your way then you're in for a very tough time of it. Personally I never speak badly of anyone, but other people have a perfect right to do or say whatever they choose. Actually, although they don't mean to, the critics spur you on, so in a strange way they're really your friends, not your enemies. All I will say is that God gave me an outstanding gift, the gift of being able to detect talent at a very young age and the ability to bring it out.'

The son of struggling Italian parents (his father ran a drugstore in the Bronx neighbourhood of New York), Bollettieri is hewn from the same rough granite as Mike Agassi: both derive great delight from bucking the system; both believe in clouting every ball as though they resented its very existence; both are unashamed self-publicists; both emerged from a world far removed from the narrow confines of the recognised tennis establishment; and their respective pupils have described both men as relentless taskmasters with mushy soft centres.

Like the boyish Emmanuel Agassi, Bollettieri stumbled across tennis almost by accident while attending Spring Hill College in Mobile, Alabama. 'The thought of going out on a tennis court had never once crossed my mind,' explains Bollettieri, who stopped by to watch two fellow army cadets trade forehands one afternoon and three months later was the unlikely star of the college team. He turned to coaching while serving as a paratrooper with the US 187th Airborne Division ('It seemed a good way to avoid route marches') and continued giving lessons when he completed his military service in 1954, helping to put himself through university, where he was studying criminal law, by charging $1.50 an hour.

Despite the deep misgivings of his parents, by that time Bollettieri had long decided that his future lay not in a courtroom but on the tennis court, even though he was fully aware he did not harbour the remotest prospect of making any sort of living as a full-time professional player. After he dropped out of law school, there followed a carefree period spent hitching his way around Latin America, before he finally talked his way into a job as coach at a top Miami hotel resort. Though he displayed a natural flair for teaching, Bollettieri knew little of the technicalities involved and had to continue taking coaching lessons himself in order to learn about different grips, swings, service actions, tactics, etc.

It was during these happy-go-lucky summers among the fractious juveniles and the face-lifted geriatrics who formed the daily queue for lessons that he gradually became convinced he could utilise whatever coaching ability he possessed plus his marine corps background to produce a tennis world champion. 'The more I thought about the obvious similarities between coaching and military training, the more I came to see that an academy set-up could work. You see, individuals really do believe they can become better in their chosen field if cast in a group setting.'

In 1958 he launched his first project, a sort of travelling circus of young coaches which traversed the country. For twelve years he spent the summer months teaching in the United States and the winter as head coach in a Puerto Rican hotel. And there, had he not happened upon a remarkably gifted ten-year-old boy from Baltimore, his career might have stagnated.

Over the next two decades, Brian Gottfried won twenty-five Grand Prix singles titles, four Grand Slam doubles championships including the Wimbledon trophy in 1976 with Mexican Raul Ramirez, and became a regular member of the American Davis Cup squad. But Gottfried's emergence as a top-ten player served only to make his go-ahead coach even more determined to discover, shape and polish a future Wimbledon singles champion. In 1975, by which time Gottfried was climbing to a ranking of third in the world behind Jimmy Connors and Bjorn Borg, the Nick Bollettieri Tennis Academy opened in Bradenton with a staff of ten and a live-in student body of thirty (today the ratio is usually around 130/225).

Overnight, the school attracted an intimidating reputation for rigid parade ground discipline. Bollettieri's lengthy and detailed rule book forbade smoking, drinking, swearing, escaping over the wall (students are allowed to leave the grounds only with the written permission of the 'camp commandant') or using drugs, all of which bring instant expulsion. Walking on the grass incurs a $5 spot fine, as does chewing gum. The fine for entering another student's room is $25, and each inmate is permitted to watch one television programme and make just one telephone call a week.

A typical working day begins at 5.45 a.m. with a 3-mile run along the paradise island beach, the making up and cleaning out of beds and dormitories, four hours of concentrated academic lessons at the nearby Bradenton Academy, 2½ hours of tennis practice, followed by foot drills, press-ups, chin-lifts, and 1½ hours of mandatory written homework before lights out at 10.30 p.m. sharp. On Saturdays and Sundays the students are free to do as they wish – unless Bolettieri's brood are engaged in a tournament, which is usually the case for about forty weeks of the year.

There are 24-hour security patrols, random checks by police sniffer dogs and a communal dining-hall which serves only the healthiest of health foods. 'Yes, I'm afraid it's true, we did run the school on the lines of a marine boot camp,' admits Bollettieri, who has now relaxed his rules and regulations very slightly, even the most controversial one which called for the withholding of water bottles for on-court misdemeanours. 'Don't forget I was a paratrooper and the military was the only way of life I knew. On top of that, a lot of the parents wanted their children to have such discipline instilled in them.'

It may come as a surprise, but not everyone found fault with the regime, and the academy staff are happy to produce files bulging with evidence of their successes in the form of glowing testimonials from delighted parents who saw such discipline as a return to those heady pre-permissive days of the 1950s. 'My son was a spoiled, pampered, overweight fourteen-year-old brat with long hair and a short temper,' wrote an ecstatic company president, 'with no respect for himself or others. Now he is trim physically, and fit emotionally. You have our deepest appreciation and heartfelt thanks.'

Such appreciation and heartfelt thanks does not come cheap. Bollettieri's annual fee for the nine-month term, which runs from September to May, is $19,500 inclusive of tennis tuition, food and lodging, plus an additional $6,000 for academic lessons. At any one time there will be at least five students receiving full scholarships (Andre Agassi was one such), with another fifteen or so receiving free tennis instruction while paying for their room and board.

But despite the successes of Agassi and Monica Seles, who was to leave the academy amid much mutual mud-slinging, the general feeling across most of America remains one of deep misgiving. 'For a twelve-year-old, where's the fun or what's the point in whacking tennis balls all day from a line of supermarket trollies?' demands one rival coach, while the US Tennis Association president David Markin, pointing out the preponderance of coaches Bollettieri hires from Mexico and beyond, dismisses the worth of an academy where much of the day is spent 'hitting backhands against faceless South Americans'. Another former USTA official, who simply refuses, on aesthetic grounds, to watch Courier in action describes the typical Bollettieri player thus: 'As subtle as a bull's fart. Huge exaggerated forehand, two-fisted topspin backhand, serviceable serve, and non-existent volley. It's like the Demolition Derby with tennis nets.'

As if in answer to such criticism, Bollettieri's questionable methods gained immediate credence. One summer no fewer than thirty of his youthful protégés littered the men's and women's Wimbledon singles championships, while three of his earliest students – Jimmy Arias, Aaron Krickstein and Carling Bassett – all soared up the world rankings in spectacular fashion. By the time he was nineteen, Arias had reached number five in the world, the seventeen-year-old Krickstein achieved seventh spot, and Bassett stood eighth among the women at the age of eighteen. But if the trio's ascendancy was quick, their decline was stunningly swift. Arias, winner of the Italian Open and a US Open semi-finalist in 1983, plunged to a dismal 106th on the computer, Krickstein, plagued by injuries to his wrists, feet and knees, plummeted even further, and Bassett dropped out of the women's top 150, thereby finding herself having to pre-qualify for the US Open, an event in which she had contested the semi-finals in 1984. Just three of countless such invalids, so claimed the critics, suffering from 'Bollettieri burn-out'. McEnroe called them 'victims'.

Krickstein, who in 1983 became the youngest-ever winner on the men's tour when he won the Tel Aviv Grand Prix two months past his sixteenth birthday, is now rebuilding his career without Bollettieri's guidance, and claims he should have been encouraged to work on his shortcomings rather than concentrate on his strengths. 'If we had worked more on my volleying and general net game when I was sixteen, who knows what I might have achieved. But since I was winning, I just kept playing the way I knew best. In the short term it paid dividends, but it was blinkered thinking.'

Arias, too, has flirted with repeated comebacks, even though he says quietly: 'Right now I'd love to have a nine-to-five job. There was a time when I walked on court wanting to get right back off.' Now twenty-eight, Arias is equally brutal about his ability as a player. 'My father told me I was a bum, Bollettieri told me I was great. He gave me absolute confidence. I wasn't pretty to watch, though, I just got the ball back and ran like a madman. I still play the same way I did as an eleven-year-old – though I guess I have more fun now.'

As with his regulations, Bollettieri gradually eased back on the coaching methods he had employed in the making of the Krickstein–Arias–Bassett generation, slashing the hours spent on the practice court from six to less than three per day. 'Sure, we made mistakes, to that I openly confess. Looking back to those early days it's easy to see how we may have sacrificed fun for the sake of competition. But the whole atmosphere at the academy has undergone big changes since then. Now my pupils develop together as a group, keeping the individual element very low in our priorities. I guess over the years I've learned how to instil discipline without deflating the kids' egos or making them feel any less of a person in the eyes of the other students. In the beginning I was too dogmatic, but I still honestly believe there has to be pressure. Life *is* pressure, wouldn't you say?'

Though now into his sixties, Bollettieri, who sports a Hollywood suntan (on overcast days he spends at least one hour lying on a sunbed) and habitually dresses like Agassi's younger brother in tee-shirt, daringly brief purple shorts and colour-coordinated Dame Edna Everage sunglasses, remains a walking, talking advertisement for his own methods. He sleeps only five hours a day, bristles with good health, spends anything up to three of his nineteen waking hours working out in the gym, and the rest of his day making deals and champions. Irrespective of age, women are routinely addressed as 'dear', men as 'sir', and frequent thanks are given unto God.

'We have a factory here in Bradenton and every three years or so we turn out a world-class player. That's how the system works, a lot of hard work, and with a lot of help from God. I've given so much to the children, you know, working eighteen or nineteen hours a day, seven days a week, 365 days a year. I'm always available for parents to see me or to call me up for a progress report. You know how long it has taken me to reach where I am? Thirty-five years. I am not a god, no sir, but the answer to your question, "Who made Jim Courier or Monica Seles?" must be their mothers and Nick Bollettieri.'

The regular references to Courier and Seles are cited as if by way of exorcism, for both were contemporaries of Agassi's at the academy before making highly publicised withdrawals after growing increasingly jealous at the amount of time Bollettieri devoted to his star pupil.

Courier, who would win two French Opens and the Australian championship before Agassi's 1992 Wimbledon triumph, might have enjoyed a successful career as a baseball pitcher had he not decided to turn his back on the sport which was his first love at the age of thirteen to concentrate solely on tennis. 'I knew I had a chance, albeit an outside one, of being one of the world's best tennis player. No way was I ever going to be the best pitcher, so there really wasn't any choice,' clarifies Courier, who is seldom seen off court without his Cincinatti Reds' baseball cap.

After Agassi turned professional immediately following his sixteenth birthday on 1 May 1986, Courier became aware he was little more than a second-class citizen in the eyes of Bollettieri, whom, so he believed, was spending a disproportionate amount of time away from the camp in Bradenton to follow his young charge around the world. 'It wasn't that Nick disregarded Jim,' explains Courier's one-time coach Sergio Cruz, the former Portuguese Davis Cup player, 'but he was convinced in his own mind that Agassi was a sure-fire number one. Bollettieri thought that although Courier might make a good living he was extremely unlikely ever to win a Grand Slam, say. From that point of view, you can hardly blame him for concentrating so much time and energy on Andre.'

Though they were originally room-mates at the academy, Courier and Agassi were by no means soul-mates and although their mutual antipathy never led to actual fisticuffs, the arguments and insults were many and inventive. 'We were both very different back then, and I'd have to say we're still pretty different now,' adds Courier, who derived immense personal satisfaction from his 3–6, 6–4, 2–6, 6–1, 6–4 defeat of Agassi in the final of the 1991 French Open in Paris. Matters had come to a head in 1989 when the two Bradenton students faced one another across the net in Philadelphia and Bollettieri, who was still Courier's official personal coach at the time, sat beside Phil Agassi and made no secret of where his enthusiastic support lay.

When the same thing happened a few months later during the US Hardcourt Championship at Forest Hills, New York, Courier, deeply hurt by what he felt was a calculated betrayal, flounced out of the academy in the company of Cruz silently vowing revenge. His vengeance was both swift and sweet. In the third round of the 1989 French Open in May, Courier outlasted his bitter adversary in four gruelling sets. At the end he hurled his racquet high into the air and cast an understandably smug smile at Bollettieri and the rest of the shell-shocked

Agassi entourage sitting en masse in the front row of the bullring-shaped number one court at Roland Garros.

Like Courier, Serbian Monica Seles was also to quit Bollettieri's before attaining the coveted number one spot on the world rankings list, in spite of having been cast in the role of head girl opposite Agassi's head boy at the academy from the moment she and her family alighted in Florida from their home among the noxious factory chimneys of Novi Sad. So ardent had Bollettieri been in the wooing of Seles, whom he had first seen as a spindly eleven-year-old winning the 1985 Orange Bowl (the junior age-group world championships), that her parents Karolj and Esther, plus her elder brother Zoltan, were all brought over to Bradenton from eastern Europe and ensconced in a luxurious bungalow overlooking the beach.

Once settled under the Florida sun, the family Seles was cosseted as none before. Not even Agassi was to enjoy such a wealth of privileges; Karolj, Esther and Zoltan were provided with transport and allowed free run of the tennis camp, while Monica practised behind a huge green curtain to keep her safe from prying eyes. 'In my thirty-odd years in the game,' Bollettieri was to say, 'I've never seen anyone like her. There was only one thing on her mind even as a tiny tot, to be number one in the world. Number two never meant anything to her.'

Predictably, the split, when it came in early 1990, was a bloody one, Monica Seles belittling Bollettieri's efforts by saying: 'Nick was never really my coach, you know. My father has always been in charge of my coaching. He's the one who taught me everything I know. Sure I stayed at the academy, but it was my father who supervised my practice.' For his part, Bollettieri appeared at times to be close to tears in Paris that same May during the French Open at Roland Garros when watching his sixteen-year-old former pupil win the first of her many Grand Slam championships. 'For two years I fed the family. For two years I clothed them. For two years they had a car to take them wherever they wanted to go. Neither

Monica nor her parents nor her brother wanted for anything. And in all that time I never took a penny off them. Not once. I coached her and I taught her. Now if I wasn't Monica's coach, then please tell me what I was, sir.'

On the few occasions when Seles's and Agassi's paths had crossed at the academy, they would share a coke and a laugh – or a gripe – which is more than the cocky Agassi ever enjoyed with his erstwhile room-mate Courier. David Wheaton, who continues to live in the intimidating shadows of his fellow-graduates (his main claim to fame being that his quarter-final victory of 1991 means he is the last man to have beaten Agassi at Wimbledon), befriended both, even though he finds it difficult to recall an occasion when they, in turn, exchanged more than the most cursory of greetings. The mutual animosity between Agassi and Courier was deep-felt and immediate, and, whatever their public protestations to the contrary these days, lasting.

Whereas Agassi hailed from the bright lights of Las Vegas some 3,000 miles away, Courier was born but a ninety-minute drive away from Bradenton in Dade City (which he still half jokingly refers to as Dead City) where his father Jim is a company executive in an orange juice factory and his mother Linda is a retired schoolteacher; whereas Agassi was reared among the casinos and show biz personalities of the Strip, Courier delivered groceries and had a paper round; whereas Agassi was rebellious, flamboyant and outspoken, Courier, four months younger but light-years less street-smart, was courteous, artless and quietly intelligent; whereas Agassi had been taught to play tennis by his macho father Mike, Courier had been taught by his great-aunt Emma; whereas Agassi had looked like a champion-in-waiting from the age of four, Courier looked as though he would never be anything other than an honest pro; whereas Agassi was already turning the heads of teenage girls, the only thing the red-haired, fair-skinned, befreckled Courier turned was lobster pink in the sun.

'Dade City is a very small town, full of very simple people,' describes Courier, not without affection for his birthplace. 'Unlike New York or Las Vegas, it's not what you would call "crowded". In fact, the whole atmosphere is low key and open. Everyone is very friendly and they just sort of go along at their own pace whatever that might be. My family certainly wasn't wealthy like some of the guys' families are, but neither were we poor. So I didn't need to do jobs as a kid, it was just kinda fun, like playing baseball and soccer and tennis and going to school.

'I guess every waking non-school moment was spent outside in the fresh air playing sports. We didn't have Nintendo, we didn't have a video recorder. Where I came from we had three channels on the television and the cartoons went off at four o'clock in the afternoon. The best thing about my parents is that they gave me a lot of independence, that's why I don't need a whole gang around me all the time. And although they never imposed themselves upon me, they gave me a good set of ethics and morals. My dad and mom certainly aren't ostentatious and I wasn't raised to be ostentatious either.'

Even as a youngster at Bollettieri's, Courier refused to act 'like a star', behaving with exactly the same courtesy and modesty as would be expected at home. 'I don't change for anybody or anything. I think I'm a very pleasant person and always have been. But if people are unpleasant to me, then I am capable of being unpleasant back. I've always been the type of guy who doesn't forget, and there's no doubt I can be very vindictive if need be. If you're my enemy, I'll go to any lengths to bury you.'

Strangely, despite his upbringing and calm demeanour, the young Courier had to learn to tame a fiery on-court temperament and his first coach at Bollettieri's remembers him as a 'scarlet-topped firebrand, always yelling, screaming and kicking at fences'.

For his part, David Wheaton, already something of an oddity in that he arrived at Bollettieri's as a classic serve-volleyer, appeared to be an even less likely superstar in the making.

Like Agassi and Courier, long before he had turned fifteen Wheaton had simply run out of suitable opposition of any age, which is why, after much soul-searching, his parents Bruce and Mary Jane reached the painful conclusion that their son would be better off with Bollettieri in Bradenton than mopping up his so-called rivals in Minnesota. Understandably perhaps, the Wheatons did not relish the prospect of their youngest child (sister Marnie is an air stewardess, while brothers Mark and John form a more than adequate doctor-lawyer partnership on the tennis court) living in an eight-bunk cell block, however comfortable it might be, with seven other strange teenagers.

As with Seles, Bollettieri rewrote his rule book, allowing Wheaton a room of his own in the cottage used by Aaron Krickstein, who was then the academy's star pupil. The son of a pathologist and grandson of a rabbi, Krickstein is one of the nicest – and quietest – players on the tour. Wheaton became inconsolably homesick, and at Bollettieri's encouragement the youngster's parents rented out the family home in Minneapolis and moved to Florida. The deeply religious Mary Jane Wheaton would later have a dramtic effect on the life of Andre Agassi.

The three fresh arrivals settled into this strange, new environment at Bollettieri's. Wheaton studied hard at school, practised hard on the court, and spent what free time there was reading the Bible; Courier, an exemplary pupil both in the classroom and on the tennis court, disciplined mind and body with ruthless single-mindedness, and relaxed by playing his guitar and drum kit or by reading the works of Roger Angell, Roger Kahn and Thomas Boswell, three of America's greatest baseball writers; Agassi threw racquets and tantrums, and turned to alcohol, marijuana and wilful disobedience.

The first piece of news to wing its way back to Las Vegas caused unrestrained celebrations. Bolletteri had taken one look at Agassi going through his paces on the practice court and immediately awarded him a full scholarship. Henceforth, therefore, his coaching, education, food, clothing, racquets and other equipment would all be provided completely free of charge.

Bollettieri, whose troubled private life has included four wives (he married the last, Kellie, when she was still in her twenties) and brought him five children who now range in age from thirty-five years to twenty-four months, admits his 'generosity of spirit has caused all sorts of problems'. 'There is no use me denying it's been hard on all my wives. One of them had been with me less than four months and suddenly she found herself sharing a house with twelve children she'd never seen before. You must understand that all the pupils who come to Bradenton are my children, though I obviously can't let every one of them stay for free. You can only do that for the very special ones otherwise you won't last five minutes.' Bollettieri eventually sold the financial control of his school to Mark McCormack's International Management Group (IMG) in January 1988 for around $2 million.

'Jim Courier was with us here in Florida for five years and he never paid me a dime. Tim Mayotte [a former Wimbledon semi-finalist] was here for a while and paid nothing. Monica Seles and her family – nothing. I've never asked anyone for anything. Carling Bassett's father gave the academy a mini-bus, our first, in fact, and God bless Mr Bassett, I say. And I also remember Mr Krickstein donated a wonderful piano. But Andre is the first player who ever gave me anything back in financial terms. He was special as a boy, and he's proved himself to be a very special young man. A special player, and a special person.'

Nor was Bollettieri alone in believing that the brash young Nevadan who first descended upon him ten years ago was something out of the ordinary. 'Even as a thirteen-year-old Andre was hitting the ball as well as any of the pros,' recalls Aaron Krickstein, 'that is very cleanly, forehand and backhand, and with an incredible amount of power. He always had the talent, but I'd have to say he was a spunky little kid who did a lot of really weird things. He always seemed determined to land himself in trouble. He had a fiery temper, too, but you kinda felt there was no limit to what he would achieve in the game if he could just quieten down and behave like any normal kid. But Andre was never what you would call "normal", and maybe that's why he's had such success.'

With anything up to 250 full-time and visiting students from over forty-five countries on 'campus' at any given time, Bollettieri has long been aware that any hint of scandal, the merest whiff of impropriety would spell disaster. Accordingly, he ran the academy (and Agassi) more on the lines of a Benedictine monastery than a hippy commune, though unlike the Bradenton students it is doubtful if the good monks would ever have to endure sporadic raids by specially trained drug sniffing police dogs.

'The parents who send their children to me are entrusting me with their spiritual and physical well-being,' explains Bollettieri righteously. 'We have all the problems you would expect at an English boarding school and there is no doubt the most difficult part of the whole business comes when the lights are switched out at ten-thirty. That's why we have to employ a complete back-up staff to work evenings, plus a team of security guards operating in pairs on constant patrol.

'When you have so many teenagers crammed together under one roof, as it were, there are obviously times when we are confronted with one or more of the problems associated with young people in the 1990s – sex, drugs and alcohol. Though I can put my hand on my heart and say such occasions have been very, very rare, believe me. Everyone who comes here knows and accepts the rules. They realise any infringement, no matter how seemingly trivial, means instant expulsion. Naturally, we have room checks, what large school doesn't? We have to be seen to be operating everything properly. We owe that to the parents, wouldn't you say? I like to tell the kids, "Drugs give you the wings to fly,/Then they take away the sky."

'It's certainly a round-the-clock 24-hours-a-day job. When a young man or woman enters my office and asks for a job as an instructor, counsellor or whatever, there's one sure-fire way for them to terminate the interview before it has even started. "Coach, what are my hours?" are those fatal words if you want to know.'

Hy Zausner, a one-time associate of Bollettieri's in New York, reacts to suggestions that many students may become depressed and suicidal by saying: 'If the kid concerned can handle the stuff Nick hands out, he's going to be okay. But if he can't he's gonna be crushed.'

As well as receiving saturation academic and tennis lessons, Bollettieri's students are also given regular counselling on drug and alcohol abuse, and sex and contraception by professional experts brought in from outside. Andre Agassi must have skipped classes.

Thousands of miles away from home, separated from his family and his small but close-knit circle of friends, Agassi wasted no time in venting all his teenage frustration, all his teenage rebellion on Bollettieri and his accursed marine corps discipline. He escaped more often than Houdini, he consumed quantities of beer, he experimented with marijuana (he is now one of sport's loudest critics of drug abuse), and generally behaved like a boorish punk. 'McEnroe in diapers,' says one former academy instructor, 'though you got the feeling it was all an act of some sort.'

Despite his obvious prowess with a tennis racquet, the petulant, posturing rebel failed to make an impact in the many tournaments in which he was entered, which brought on him the wrath of his father in Las Vegas and the patent disapproval of his equally hard-to-please tutor. Mike Agassi had come to believe his son should win every match he played, preferably 6–0, 6–0, while Bollettieri grew increasingly impatient at his young troublemaker's apparent fascination with the personal self-detonation button he carried around with him.

When not testing the elasticity of Bollettieri's rigid rules, Agassi enjoyed seeing just how far he could throw a racquet or, even better, how quickly he could reduce it to a mangled pile of twisted graphite. By night he would dress himself in black from head to toe and engage in childish acts of mini-vandalism around campus; by day he would curse and swear and behave in such an anti-social manner that he was invariably made to practise on some out-of-the-way court where his rage horrified even the most experienced teaching pros. 'He had,' as one instructor observed, 'what you could call an attitude problem. And you can put those two words in lights. No one wanted to work with him, except Nick, that is.

'Bollettieri might not be the most accomplished tennis coach in the world, but I'd have to say he must be the most loyal. Even when Andre was at his worst, and believe me Andre's worst is just about as bad as you can get, he stuck by the kid as if he were his own son. We all knew what Andre was up to, the beer, the pot, the trips downtown, but Nick just carried on with the job he'd started. To build himself a Wimbledon champion.'

'You know, they're right. I was just so obnoxious,' is how Agassi describes his former self during those troubled teenage years in Florida. 'A real headcase, you could say. I was so lonely, no one will ever know just how lonely. I suppose that's the perverse reason I continually tried to make it even tougher on myself by constantly getting into trouble of some sort.'

While Agassi was running wild long after the academy's supposed 10.30 p.m. lights out, on court he was behaving like a vandal, hurling racquets high over the back fence into the parents-only swimming pool, or smashing them to smithereens against the nearest fixed object. After one particularly galling defeat, Agassi remembers 'trashing all seven racquets I had in my bag against the side of a building. But I didn't know any different, that's the way my life always used to be as a kid.'

All told, Agassi reckons he was demolishing an average of forty Prince racquets a year (ironically it is his present racquet manufacturer Donnay which has enjoyed the massive fruits of its client's successes) to the unrestrained amusement of his fellow scholars, many of whom looked upon him as a heroically rebellious figure of their generation, others as a mere hoodlum. 'He was a punk, a brat, a maniac, or whatever you want to call him,' says Alicia Hernandez, who at fifteen spent a week in Bradenton before scuttling home to the security of her parents in Guadalajara and on to a finishing school in Switzerland. 'He could have been real cute, if he hadn't been so disagreeable – and if he hadn't looked so weird all the time. But you got the feeling it was all just an act, that he was demanding attention and approval by screaming "LOOK AT ME!"'

Agassi's penchant for the outrageous had already taken hold and, ever eager to shock his band of admirers and critics alike, he began appearing in a monthly succession of outlandish hairstyles. 'It all started for a bet with this other kid called Ty Tucker. You know the kind of thing: "Go on, I bet you, if you shave your head, I'll shave mine". Anyway, he did, and so I did.' Agassi then allowed his crewcut, actually more of a 'shaven Hare-Krishna', to blossom into a 'full Mohican', at which point the principal teacher at Bradenton High School attempted to call a halt to the proceedings. 'He told me if I did anything else to my hair, other than to let it grow in an acceptable manner, I'd be expelled.' Agassi proceeded directly to the nearest hairdressing salon from where, some hours later, he re-emerged with a platinum bleached-blond full Mohican.

Bored with his Indian-brave look, and as a 1985 Christmas gift to himself, Agassi then adopted an outrageous punk-style striped haircut so bizarre that even his own family hardly recognised him when he swaggered through the arrival hall of McCarran International Airport to begin his vacation. 'Whad tha hell you call that on top-a your goddam head?' spluttered an apoplectic Mike Agassi as his son succeeded in bringing unshockable Las Vegas to a standstill.

Though Rogers insists, 'Nick was furious, and Andre came

close, very, very close, to getting kicked out of the academy,'
Bollettieri is now at pains to play down such incidents, saying:
'Yes, he was on the cutting edge several times. No way did I
ever want to change his personality, though. If I had killed off
Andre's attitude, I'd have killed the champion inside him. He
was a rebel, always flamboyant, he was never what you'd call
a conformist. Mike had done a hell of a job, hitting balls with
Andre all day long, all I had to do was the fine tuning.

'Do you know the reason there are so few champions in
tennis, or any other sport for that matter? You have to take
risks to be the very best. Andre took risks. He took risks
with his life-style, and he still takes risks the way he plays.
Most people go through life without risking anything, that's
what eliminates 99.9 per cent of would-be champions. To be
the best, the very best in your chosen field, requires giving
everything.'

Despite having Bollettieri's understanding – and qualified
support – the long-delayed but inevitable showdown duly
arrived soon after when Agassi, playing quite brilliantly and
beautifully, swept through successive rounds of an important
junior tournament in Pensacola, Florida. Not content just to be
the most dazzling player on view, however, he walked out on
court to play the final wearing ripped denims, eye-liner, pink
lipstick and an earring. The crowd was stunned into silence,
and the joyous reaction of his room-mates (Courier excluded,
obviously) only hardened Bollettieri's condemnation, and the
devastating public humiliation in front of the entire staff and
student body that followed was both vigorous and extensive.

It was the excuse Agassi had been searching for ever since
he arrived in Bradenton almost three years before. Without
offering a word in his own defence, he packed his bags, stormed
through the front gates and, because Bollettieri had previously
confiscated his money and credit cards, began the long 30-mile
walk to Tampa airport. Bollettieri, by now wise in the way of
dealing with teenage tantrums, allowed Agassi a good two-hour

start before overhauling him in the academy mini-bus. He and the would-be runaway then aired their respective grievances to one another while closeted together for over two hours in his private office.

'Sometimes you don't appreciate how tough it is on us kids here,' Agassi told the older man seriously. 'You forget how much is expected of us, how much is demanded. We're just kids, you know. Most of us are lonely, most of us are far away from home. Maybe it would help if everyone around here could just remember that every once in a while.' Moved by the sincerity of his words – and the complete lack of any apparent self-pity – Bollettieri softened and resolved to give his multi-talented tearaway another chance, even though it was to be some time before he could detect any discernible change in Agassi's attitude on and off court. 'Looking back now, I was darned lucky not to get into a fight every time I went out on court to play,' admits Agassi. 'I tended to be very critical of my opponents, especially if I was losing. And anyway, I had discovered that the madder I got, the better I played.'

This bully-boy approach may have worked to devastating effect against his adolescent contemporaries, but it almost earned him a black eye when making his debut appearance in a professional tournament as a fifteen-year-old. Agassi's first-round opponent was the tough Serbian Marko Ostoja, a wily campaigner of twenty-seven with an ingrained dislike of being on the wrong end of any gamesmanship which might be flying around. As a schoolboy who had come through the qualifying tournament into the main draw, Agassi might have been expected to treat his opponent, a seasoned player then ranked in the top 100, with a modicum of respect. Not so.

Fully aware of Ostoja's fragile temperament, Agassi queried the legality of a thumping service winner which had clearly bounced inside the line and demanded that the line judge involved reverse his call. As the argument raged back and forth between Agassi, umpire and linesman, Ostoja finally cracked and began arguing his case in a steadily rising voice from the other side of the court. 'Why don't you shut up and just stay out of this!' bellowed Agassi. At which point the tempestuous Serbian duly shut up, stretched across the net and delivered unto Agassi a painful and resounding smack on the cheek.

Mostly, however, it was Agassi who meted out the strong-arm tactics, and he rapidly gained a reputation on the junior tournament circuit for deliberately smashing easy returns directly at his opponents' head or stomach (or, more painfully, slightly lower). 'He was definitely a bit of a punk,' says Courier without the slightest hint of reluctant admiration in his voice. 'Everyone knows he was never much of a student at the academy, and if he'd continued on the same path he'd have gone down the toilet.'

If all this gives the impression Agassi had been abandoned by wolves and brought up by his parents, Rogers, speaking in his friend's defence, understandably interprets things somewhat differently. 'The clothes, the hair, the behaviour were all pure rebellion. Andre was just letting a few people know he was not entirely happy with the way his life was going. I don't want to make it sound like some huge sob story, because Andre was brought up with a lot more advantages than most kids, but there wasn't a lot of stability. He was thousands of miles away from home, from his girlfriend and his best friend, and that can make you pretty unhappy. His childhood was pretty much taken away from him at the academy in certain respects.

'Any fool could see what was happening. Whenever Andre came home he'd watch me whooping it up with the old gang and it reminded him what he was missing out on being stuck out there in Bradenton. I think he was scared, scared he was going through a living hell just to be a tennis player. And what if he didn't make it? He was terrified he wouldn't succeed, and what then? As a safeguard, he sort of joked around, as if to say, "Look. It doesn't matter, it really doesn't. I don't care if I make it or not."'

'I did miss out on a lot,' agrees Agassi. 'But I knew I could always talk to Perry whenever I needed to be reminded of what it's like to be a normal teenager.' Though Bollettieri permitted his students only one phone call home a week, Agassi became adept at slipping unnoticed past the guards on the front gate to find a call box from which he would conduct a two-hour long-distance conversation with his friend back home in Las Vegas.

Ironically, Rogers had been given first-hand experience of his buddy's over-aggressive nature as an eleven-year-old during an inconsequential local event in Las Vegas. When Agassi took an unexpectedly severe beating in an early round, the thoughtful Rogers sought out the disconsolate stranger to offer a few quiet words of sympathy. 'And who the hell do you think you are?' snapped Andre the Ungracious. 'I told a mutual friend I wasn't too impressed with Andre's manners and obviously word got back.' A couple of days later Rogers received an invitation to accompany Agassi to the movies and the pair have been inseparable ever since.

Rogers, who now studies at the University of Arizona, was an undistinguished tennis player as a junior, but that did not deter Agassi from entering his newly-acquired friend's name in all the major tournaments in which he himself was competing. On one occasion Agassi even persuaded Bollettieri to pull all manner of strings to gain his closest confidant an offer to compete in a prestigious national championship being played in Florida. Not content with that, Agassi then sold all the tennis clothes he had just been given by one of his clothing sponsors to pay for his less fortunate friend's first-class airline ticket to and from Tampa.

Even now, Rogers is likely to return from his university lectures to discover a box of his favourite fried chicken segments sitting on his desk, arranged by Agassi in conjunction with Tramps, the duo's long-time favourite fast-food diner in Las Vegas.

'That's Andre all over,' says Rogers. 'If he decides to love you he's generous almost to a fault. I really don't think there's anything he wouldn't do for his friends or family, which is why I get so angry when I read or hear any criticism of Andre coming from someone who's never met the guy or who barely knows him. There are two Andres really, the glamorous, tempestuous one you see on court or in the TV adverts, and the kind, considerate one who you only get to see if he allows you.'

Bollettieri and Mike Agassi have also been recipients of Andre's whims of largess, both being handed the keys to $100,000 sports cars as a 'token of my appreciation for what you've done for me'. 'Yes, he takes care of his old coach,' smiles Bollettieri. 'And not because I've asked him. I've never asked Andre for anything, no sir, but, yes, he did buy me a new car a couple of Christmases back.'

To the world at large, however, the sixteen-year-old Agassi continued his havoc wreaking ways, even incurring the wrath of his home state supporters in the Nevada Open played in Reno in May 1986. After spending five weeks criss-crossing the nation on the satellite circuit, the Reno event was not a tournament tennis's newest professional would have voluntarily entered. He did so only to please elder brother Phil, who, still hopeful of joining the pro ranks himself, was desperately keen to win the doubles title. Being forced to perform against his will brought out the worst in Agassi and he horrified those fellow-Nevadans who had come to praise him with his language, near-perfect racquet throwing technique, insulting of opponents by making obscene gestures, by thrusting the racquet between his legs, and generally making John McEnroe look like Mary Poppins in comparison.

Agassi may have won the tournament, but he had lost the affection of the crowd long before they applauded a particularly outstanding volley by his opponent in the final. 'SHUT UP!' screamed Agassi, disgusted that the spectators should dare display such a sporting reflex action.

Dr Cary Fenton, one of the organisers of the Nevada Open seven years ago, admits to being 'sickened' by what he saw.

'He was the classic American brat, big-headed, spoiled, ignorant and rude. You name it and Andre Agassi was "it". Everyone who was there that week had either seen or heard McEnroe, but this was something else again. He behaved hideously and I think people only kept coming in the hope of seeing him beaten. I'm almost certain his friends and supporters can offer all sorts of diferent excuses and come up with all kinds of psychological reasons for the way Agassi was as a sixteen-year-old, but to me they're baloney, to use a polite word. He was a foul-mouthed thug who'd obviously been allowed to run wild. I don't remember coming across any kid – not even the ones from the toughest ghettos – that ever treated other people with such contempt. I've never met him since, in fact I still refuse to watch him, even on television.

'He may have won the Wimbledon championship, but he'll never be a champion to anyone who saw him that time in Reno.' Like Agassi and Courier, Alexander Sutherland was just another anonymous hopeful on the southern Californian junior tournament treadmill in the mid-1980s, but one who, in his own estimation, 'was never going to be the best player in my street, let alone the best player in the world.' 'But I was enjoying myself and having fun,' says Sutherland, now studying to be a veterinary surgeon in Boston. 'After a week of school classes it was nice to spend the weekends outdoors, hanging out at some tennis club. Occasionally, and I do mean occasionally, I'd even win a match or two, but mostly I lost, like love-and-love in the first round.

'I learned that even losing has its compensations, though. Since there were always lots of pretty girls hanging about, the quicker you lost, then the more time you had to kinda chat them up.

'But I eventually stopped playing altogether because of Andre Agassi and his like, even though I never actually got to play him in a serious match. It was his whole attitude which put me off, his arrogance, his ruthlessness, his temper. I once read a description of John McEnroe which said he was "possessed by the Furies". Well, that phrase suited the Agassi I used to see to a T.

'I wasn't a goody-goody, but my parents brought me up to consider other people's feelings. I was taught the whole "do unto others bit". My recollections of Andre Agassi are those of a mean-spirited little guy who would swear and shout and stamp his feet till he got his own way. Seeing him act that way put me off, it really did. And that's why I just stopped playing competitively. I didn't mind losing every week, I just hated being in that kind of "win-at-all-costs" atmosphere.

'It's seems odd when I see him on television now. He seems so well-behaved, so careful not to cause offence, that I expect him to crack at any minute and start screaming his head off like in the old days. There was no way I couldn't watch the Wimbledon final, though I admit my fiancée Martha and I were rooting for the other guy. I've known Agassi for such a long time that I've become fascinated by him. I read every article, buy every magazine with his face on the cover, study every advertisement, and go to the US Open at Flushing Meadow every summer.

'Once I stood next to him when he was signing autographs and really felt tempted to say, "Hi, Andre. You won't remember me but we shared a locker room in Redondo Beach, Ventura, Laguna or wherever." It's funny to think the same skinny kid with the funny haircut that I knew is now just about the most famous athlete in the world. Maybe I was jealous, I know a lot of the other guys playing the juniors back then were, but I honestly don't think so. I just don't think he was very likeable. The people who should know say he's different now and I'd be really curious to know when and how this complete personality change took place.'

Dr James E. Loehr, sports psychologist and Director of Sports Science for the USTA, has been called 'the single most important person in tennis today' by the late Arthur

Ashe, Wimbledon champion in 1975 and one of the most respected voices in American sport. The author of ten instructional books and two videos, Dr Loehr, who has helped Martina Navratilova and Monica Seles, among others, worked at the Bollettieri Academy during Agassi's formative years and remembers him as being the 'type who would throw racquets, tantrums, and quit under pressure. Andre was driven, moody, angry, temperamental, edgy, nervous. Now he's a player of poise and perspective, maturity, unpredictability, sportsmanship, humour and mental toughness.'

And the reason for this sudden and dramatic metamorphosis? In ascending order, Dr Loehr, Nick Bollettieri and God.

Agassi had attended the the First Good Shepherd Lutheran school in Las Vegas in his pre-teens, but his knowledge of the Bible was skimpy and he had not given religion any thought for some years until Mary Jane Wheaton (mother of David) engaged him in conversation during a pause in the academy's frantic curriculum one afternoon in 1987. 'Andre, do you know where you'll go when you die?' she challenged. Agassi, then seventeen, had no idea, but the seriousness of the enquiry persuaded him to seek out the help of Fritz Glauss, the travelling vicar on the men's tennis tour, and their resultant conversations, often long and heated, became a regular sideshow to the usual locker-room discussions about 'sex, drugs and rock 'n' roll'. 'Fritz earned my trust. I was facing a lot of questions in my life because I knew there just had to be more important things in life than tennis, fame and money. I thought I'd give the Bible a chance.'

In the company of Glauss, Mrs Wheaton and Michael Chang, Agassi began taking part in daily Bible readings and prayer group meetings, before converting to Christianity. 'I think Andre was worried that he would be forced to give up tennis if he became a Christian,' says David Wheaton. 'But I managed to explain to him that by being a Christian you don't necessarily have to be a religious, pious kind of person, that you could still have fun and still go all out to beat your opponent on the tennis court without jeopardising your Christian principles.' Though he does not like to proclaim his religious beliefs from the pulpit, Agassi insists it was his personal God who turned his troubled life around.

'I think a lot of the criticism I'd been taking was justified. The Bible opened a new door in my life.' On his visits home to Las Vegas, Agassi also began attending the non-denominational Meadows Fellowship Church, a small chapel on the outskirts of town where pastor John Parenti, who favours long blond hair, colourful sunglasses, a huge diamond ring and, when not preaching, multi-coloured Hawaiian shorts, attracts a devoted congregation. 'I don't know that anyone has a real grasp of the pressure Andre lives under every day of his life,' explains Las Vegas's trendiest vicar. 'People expect so much of him, while every move he makes is examined microscopically. He'll call from wherever he is in the world – or drop by if he's in town – and we'll get together and try to smooth out any problems he's facing. All I can do is try to help Andre gain a biblical perspective on what's happening to him.'

But long before Agassi found God, a group of other concerned people in men's tennis were already saying their prayers.

4

The Rise of a Hero

The annual Italian championships which are played in Rome
during the first two weeks in May, have always been Ilie
Nastase's favourite halt on the tennis circuit. That should
tell you everything you need to know. When the gates of
the Foro Italico are opened on day one, it is chaos at the
jammed and impossibly narrow turnstiles. The crowds are
enormous and uncontrollable, brazenly using fists, feet, knees
and elbows to achieve the best possible standpoint – and that is
only in the seemingly never-ending line outside the wonderful
open-air trattoria, from which the inviting aroma of *spaghettini
alle vongole*, *bucatini all'Amatriciana*, and *pollo alla cacciatora*
wafts disconcertingly across the Campo Centrale (centre court).
When not hurling abuse at some luckless foreigner unfortunate
enough to have been drawn to play a local Italian, or much
worse as Bjorn Borg once discovered when he ill-advisedly
defeated Adriano Panatta to an accompanying hail of coins,
the Foro fans eat, drink, flirt and argue volubly in the brilliant
sunshine. They argue about tennis, about politics, about the
respective merits of Juventus and Roma, about whether the
chef has used enough dried chilis in the *penne arrabiata*. Their

raised voices, like the smell of food, are carried far and wide on the breeze.

The Foro Italico is an assault on the senses. It looks and sounds like no other major sports stadium in the world. Built by Benito Mussolini, the beautiful arena is a magnolia-coloured marble amphitheatre comprising five clay courts the colour of dried blood surrounded by rolling hills, majestic pine trees and a circle of preposterous 30-foot statues, erected on the orders of the dictator as a monument to Italian manhood.

Silenzio per favore? Forget it. The Foro Italico masses have far more in common with a frenzied Italian football mob than the worshipful congregation which sits in devoted silence around Wimbledon's green and pleasant Centre Court. Romans, by exciting contrast to the well-behaved queues permitted entry to the All England Club, watch tennis the way they drive – without undue care and attention. They screech, collide, gesticulate, offer up muttered imprecations to the gods, cut in in front of each other without looking and hurl abuse at all around them. A great time is had by all.

Where but Rome could a linesman admit he was temporarily unsighted because he had been leaning over a hedge to buy an ice-cream during the disputed rally in question? Where but Rome could a thirteen-year-old ball boy assume an expression of genuine hurt bewilderment when informed his cigarette smoke was bothering the players? Where but Rome could a furious John McEnroe wheel round to berate an errant lineswoman and find himself drowning in the huge, limpid brown eyes of an 18-year-old Claudia Cardinale lookalike resplendent in black leather miniskirt? And where but Rome could the spectators pelt Nastase with assorted missiles then accord him a standing ovation when he hurled back an empty beer bottle?

'I love it here, they're all crazy,' beamed Nastase during last year's 1992 championships when he teamed up with his old sidekick Ion Tiriac in the over-45 veterans' doubles. 'Although I live in America most of the time these days, Rome and Paris are the two places I truly love. I enjoy the people, especially in Rome where they are like me, yes? I enjoy the food, the wine, the restaurants – and obviously the fashions,' added the Romanian, noting that female apparel is customarily worn dangerously short and tight during the two weeks of the Italian men's and women's tennis championships.

Beyond the centre court, out of sight and social range of the ordinary tennis fan, lies the patricians' playground, the private marquees and bars of the Foro Italico's tented village where the various sponsors vie with one another to provide the most glittering and exclusive gathering of the whole extravaganza. The village has long been a magnet for Roman society, businessmen, fashion models, 'wanna-be's' and off-duty tennis players such as Nastase ever since the shrewd tournament organisers persuaded a national television station to hold a live late-night chat show among the potted palms and abundant female flesh.

It was here, in the summer of 1986, that Nastase voiced his concern that the tennis boom of the 1970s was over and was being quickly followed by a grim recession. 'Take a look around the locker room. Ten years ago you would have seen Borg, Ashe, Rosewall, Orantes and Panatta,' he explained, adding with a mischievous grin, 'and maybe Nastase, of course. Great players, but also great personalities, eh? Now you have good players still, but where are the personalities? McEnroe and Connors perhaps, and that's it. And what happens when they go? Is nice that I can still start a riot whenever I play. Is nice that people still remember me but also sad, I think. Tennis needs new heroes now. A hero for the 1990s. A young player who will attract a younger audience. But not another robot. Please, we have too many robots already, don't you think?

'Is true I was wild. You know, Ceaucescu once ask me why I have to act so crazy all of the time? Is true, I promise you. I said everything I did was in the spirit of fun. Where is the fun now? The players today care only for dollars, not about having fun when out they're out there on the court. What tennis needs is another star, a superstar, and, more important, an American superstar. Europe has its champions – Becker, Edberg, Wilander, Noah, Mecir – the Australians have Pat Cash, but who do the Americans have? McEnroe is semi-retired, or so it seems, Connors is almost as old as me, though maybe Jimmy not eat so much pasta and drink so much wine? But can you see Krickstein and Arias, to use them as examples, attracting many young people to take up tennis or even come along just to watch the tournaments?'

The need for a new all-American hero was a theme also taken up by Ivan Lendl, who would go on to beat Spain's Emilio Sanchez in the final of that 1986 Italian Open. 'Compared to baseball, American football, ice hockey, basketball and golf, tennis is still not what you would call a major sport in the United States. For sure, most people will have heard of Wimbledon, and the US Open, of course, but how much publicity will the American television or newspapers devote to someone from Prague winning the Italian Open against a Spaniard? Somewhere just below the harness racing results and weather forecast. The biggest market, and by that I am talking about television and also the number of people in the world who actually go out and buy tennis racquets, shoes and clothes, is potentially in America. People in Europe either forget or don't appreciate just how big sport is across the Atlantic. The top stars are bigger than rock bands, bigger than astronauts, bigger than politicians.

'What tennis desperately needs is another American superstar. That would act as a massive boost, otherwise the TV fans will stick by the sports they're familiar with. The Americans will watch in their millions if Evert or Connors or McEnroe is playing, but it's a sad fact of life that they'll switch channels every time to find Wayne Gretzky, Carl Lewis or the New York Yankees if they turn on and discover some unknown German playing an unknown Swede in some town they've never even heard of.'

Though he came to be associated almost exclusively with the women's professional tour in his later years, the late Ted Tinling also lamented the disappearance of the 'star-system' within men's tennis. Tinling began a love affair with tennis that lasted almost seventy years when he became Suzanne Lenglen's personal umpire during a tournament in Nice in 1924, and played many and disparate roles, from couturier (he designed 'Gorgeous' Gussy Moran's infamous frilly knickers for the 1949 Wimbledon championships and Chris Evert's first wedding dress) to referee, from raconteur to provocateur, from historian to prophet, from *chef de protocole* to outrageously amusing gossipmonger.

When Ted died in a Cambridge hospital on 23 May 1990, one month before his eightieth birthday, he left behind a host of loving friends and a wealth of unerringly accurate observations. 'Women's tennis is currently in a far more exciting state of transition than the men's game,' mused Ted over the inevitable glass of champagne during the pre-Wimbledon grass court championship at Eastbourne seven summers ago. 'Martina and Chrissie's time is just about run, but here we have Graf and Sabatini ready to assume their roles centre stage plus a whole schoolroom of wonderfully talented youngsters following along right behind them. And because of Navratilova and Evert, they will all want to be princesses, little divas.

'But where, oh where, is the next generation of male stars? A Tilden, or a Gonzales, or a Hoad, or a McEnroe? I'm afraid far too many of the modern players today are content to show up, book into their pre-paid luxury hotel suites, jump into their chauffeur-driven Mercedes or whatever, play their matches, sign a couple of autographs and retire to the privacy of their rooms surrounded by a posse of faceless bodyguards. That's not how a star should behave. Whenever Tilden played half of Hollywood turned out to see him. Do you know Tallulah Bankhead, who had every man in the western world – well, just about every man, I should say – breaking out in a cold sweat, used to sit in the front row of the Centre Court during Wimbledon fortnight clutching a single red rose and without taking her eyes off him?

'Pancho Gonzales and Lew Hoad mixed with the Hollywood set, too. And like Bill Tilden they even looked like actors, better looking than most of the stars up there on the screen, in fact. Now John McEnroe's a bit different. He's not exactly what you would call the dashing screen idol type, is he? But what he does possess is charisma and an air of mystery. Why does he behave the way he does? Why does he suddenly fly into those frightful rages? Why does he seem so hell-bent on self-destruction? But then he starts to play tennis and you forgive him everything. When McEnroe is playing at the very peak of his powers it is the tennis of the gods.

'Now, you asked me what men's tennis needs and I will tell you. It needs a new star. But not just a mere tennis star. Not another anonymous athlete pounding huge service winners and ugly double-handed backhands. What it desperately needs is someone like Tilden who hits the ball cleaner and truer than anyone of his generation. Someone like Hoad with raw sex appeal. Someone like Gonzales with glamour. Someone like McEnroe with controversy.'

At that very moment in Las Vegas, many thousands of miles away from the genteel seafront of Eastbourne, where the only sounds interrupting the tennis are the cries of seagulls and the snapping of Tupperware lids, just such a figure was preparing to come out and play.

Sixteen-year-old Andre Agassi did not so much arrive on the scene in the summer of 1986 as explode upon it like an oompah band suddenly marching through the front doors of a sedate retirement home where the elderly residents are enjoying a quiet nap or a game of draughts before a cup of hot cocoa and bed.

A mere eighty-nine days after turning professional on the first day of May – and just ninety-one days after turning sixteen – he stormed through five rounds of a Challenger Series tournament (populated by young players on the way up, older players on the way down, and seasoned professionals recovering from long-term injury) in Schenectady, New York, to qualify for his first final against Indian number one Ramesh Krishnan. Krishnan, then twenty-five, had already won three important Grand Prix titles and, just two weeks earlier, had reached the quarter-finals at Wimbledon before losing to Yugoslav strong man Slobodan Zivojinovic in four sets. Once described by John McEnroe as 'a relic of a bygone age' because of the easy elegance of his strokes, Krishnan appears deceptively slow and fragile, but he is an inspired shot-maker and, already in his eighth full year on the professional circuit, knew a little bit too much for the new kid on the block.

Despite this minor setback, Agassi, who had ended 1985 ranked a lowly 618th in the world, had soared to 91st by the end of 1986. The new star Ted Tinling had despaired of sighting had been located and was rising fast.

Krishnan was among the winners on the Challenger Series circuit again in 1987, as were Michael Chang, Petr Korda, Tomas Smid, Magnus Gustafsson and Peter Doohan (the unknown Australian who would stun the tennis world by ending Boris Becker's bid for a third successive title in a second-round match on Wimbledon's number one court that summer), but Agassi had already moved on to bigger and better things. After reaching the final of the Seoul Open in late April, where he lost to American doubles specialist Jim Grabb, the seventeen-year-old burst upon the public consciousness in November by winning the South American Open in Itaparica, one of the ten richest Grand Prix events on the tour calendar outside the four great Grand Slam championships.

He had earlier given notice of his intent by qualifying for the semi-finals of two other prestigious events, at the Basle Indoor won by Yannick Noah, and at Stratton Mountain where he lost to a mightily relieved McEnroe, who noted: 'I've never played against anyone who hit the ball so hard, so often, and so accurately.'

Agassi was no longer up-and-coming, he had most certainly arrived. By the end of 1987 he was just outside the world's top twenty (at number 25 on the computer) though his pride had suffered a painful dent at Wimbledon where he had been mauled 6–2, 6–1, 6–2 by ninth-seeded Frenchman Henri Leconte in a one-sided slaughter on number two court, the so-called 'graveyard of the seeds'. Though the young American had undoubtedly looked the complete novice that he was on the uneven grass, his advisers should have striven much harder to put this heavy defeat into perspective. Leconte had been a quarter-finalist at Wimbledon in 1985 (when he defeated Ivan Lendl), a semi-finalist in 1986 (when he beat Pat Cash before losing to Boris Becker), and would go on to the last eight again in 1987 where he succumbed to Lendl in an epic return encounter.

The Frenchman, who had been playing his sixth Wimbledon championship while Agassi was making his very first appearance on an English lawn, is the most whimsical of players. Blessed with an inordinate amount of natural talent (he was the last player to defeat Bjorn Borg in serious combat, in Stuttgart in 1984), his career has been seriously hindered by a chronic back ailment. But on that sunny afternoon at Wimbledon, facing an inexperienced seventeen-year-old Agassi, he would have embarrassed any player in the world and the outcome should not have been sufficient cause to keep the vanquished teenager away from the All England Club for four years.

Despite that Wimbledon setback, however, Agassi continued to climb the world rankings, even though those wise in the way of such things insist that the most difficult step in tennis is the graduation from a 'an everyday top-twenty performer' to a top-five player. By the end of 1988, and still only eighteen, Agassi would be the third-ranked player in the world, below only Mats Wilander and Ivan Lendl, and above three past Wimbledon champions – Boris Becker, Stefan Edberg and Jimmy Connors.

'It was the kind of year a young player shouldn't even dream about,' says Agassi of those remarkable twelve months during which he won six Grand Prix titles, collected two runners-up cheques, and reached the semi-finals of both the French and US Opens. 'I guess it was what I had always prayed for since I was about six or seven, but no one really expects to wake up one morning and find himself number three in the world after such a short time on the circuit. Even now I sometimes look back at that year and think, "Phew, did I really do that?"'

Agassi's year had begun, however, with a salutary lesson that the rapier can often prove far deadlier than the broadsword. Defeat against the mesmerising Miloslav Mecir, tragically now lost to the game due to an incurable back complaint, in Rotterdam.

For a few phenomenal years in the 1980s, Mecir, frequently referred to as the 'Big Cat' because of his stealthy walk, long, lithe body and comparatively short, heavily muscled legs, was the man the other players most enjoyed watching (especially if they did not have to confront him the next day) because of his uncanny ability to make the ball appear in the most unlikely places. In fact his wizardry caused him also to be affectionately known as Merlin.

Mecir was never to win any of the four Grand Slam championships. He was a beaten finalist at both the US and Australian Opens, and would reach the semi-finals at Wimbledon in 1988, when he led Edberg by two sets to love in front of a stunned Centre Court audience before losing 4–6, 2–6, 6–4, 6–3, 6–4 to the eventual champion. His languid genius made him champion in the eyes of those who believe tennis should be a game of cunning, artistry and mischief, rather than unreturnable 120 mph service winners. It came as no surprise, therefore, to discover that Mecir's favourite form of relaxation away from the tennis circuit was angling and at the end of every major championship he would invariably bundle his wife Petra and young son Miloslav junior into his battered old Skoda and take to the breathtakingly beautiful hills of his beloved Slovakia for a lakeland fishing trip.

'Yes, fishing is exactly like tennis, I think,' mused Mecir, always far happier when discussing the one that got away than his latest tennis triumph. 'You lay the bait, then you must wait patiently to see if your rival takes the hook. I enjoyed playing tennis, and that is not as simplistic as it sounds. I liked the feel of the ball on the strings of my racquet, the sensation of creating something, of conjuring a shot out of thin air, the fun of trying something different, something no one expected. I always liked to make people smile when I played.'

Sometimes the magic vanished. On his off days, the sorcerer played like an inept apprentice. Lendl, ever the reliable Czech, was so upset by his Slovak opponent's hopeless display in the final of the 1986 US Open, which he won 6–4, 6–2, 6–0, that he apologised to the crowd at Flushing Meadow in his after-match speech.

Said Mecir: 'I know I sometimes looked bored, though I always try to do my best, I promise you. But some days, oh, I just do not know, nothing seems to work no matter what tricks I try. The balls seem heavy, like grapefruits, and the strings made out of elastic – I can't explain. Those are the days when I wish I was fishing. Those are the days when I wish I was alone in the hills.'

Karl Novacek, who was bamboozled by Mecir's wizardry more often than most during their early years in Czechoslovakia, freely admits the muscles in his stomach used to tighten up at the mere prospect of meeting this wizard on court. 'You tried to keep your eyes on the ball, but it's impossible against Milo. You look up and he is standing behind the baseline, you look up to make sure, and there he is a yard or two behind the baseline. You blink, look up again and he is on top of the net waiting to kill your return. How did he get there? No one knows. There never was and never will be anyone quite like him.'

Australian Wally Masur, a dogged serve-volleyer of the

old school who does not like surprises unless they come gift-wrapped at Christmas, memorably portrayed Mecir as 'a bloody witch-doctor', while Sweden's Mats Wilander, who later quit the sport through disenchantment, described the former Czechoslovak Davis Cup maestro as 'probably the very best player in the world when he was 100 per cent'.

Sadly for tennis and most cruelly for the Slovak – 'Lendl, Novacek and the others are Czechs, I alone am a Slovak,' he was always at pains to emphasise – Mecir's playing career was ended by a serious spinal injury despite a long, intricate and dangerous operation in Switzerland, plus a number of consultations with a plumber in his home town of Bojnice who was reputed to have 'healing hands'. Unlike the rest of his competitors, however, Mecir never once felt the need to employ a coach such as Bollettieri. 'A coach?' asks Novacek in genuine bewilderment. 'What on earth would he have wanted with a coach?'

When Agassi first confronted this magus in February 1988, Mecir, then ranked fourth in the world, used the young Las Vegan's blistering pace to reveal the full range of his trickery. By the time the match was ended, it seemed as though Agassi's hopes had disappeared in a puff of smoke, rabbits had been pulled from hats, doves were swooping overhead, and all that remained was for Mecir to saw the umpire in half.

But it is not every day you are asked to cope with the special demands of confronting a Miloslav Mecir and the following week, on 21 February 1988, Agassi won the first Grand Prix title of his short career when he beat Sweden's Mikael Pernfors in the final of the US National Indoor championships in Memphis, Tennessee.

Even in a sport cluttered with eccentrics, Pernfors has always been regarded as something of an oddball. Born in Malmo, Sweden, he went to the University of Georgia, and consequently talks with more than a hint of an American accent. He plays in an almost ungainly manner reminiscent of Groucho Marx impersonating Bjorn Borg, and has had more hairstyles than Joan Collins, let alone Agassi. In 1988 alone, Pernfors turned up for a Davis Cup tie with his hair dyed yellow and blue in a rough (very rough) approximation of the Swedish flag, played at Wimbledon in a spiky crewcut which could only have been achieved at a poodle parlour, then arrived for the US Open at Flushing Meadow, New York, in the latest greased, swept-back Gordon Gecko look made famous by Michael Douglas in the movie *Wall Street*.

Nevertheless Pernfors knew his way around a tennis court better than most, having reached the final of the French Open unseeded in 1986 when he turned over Argentine clay court master Martin Jaite, Boris Becker and Parisian heart-throb Henri Leconte in successive rounds before running into a rampant Ivan Lendl. Though he would briefly climb into the world's top ten later in the autumn of 1986, it was on the Centre Court at Wimbledon the following summer that Pernfors played his most famous match, when he led Jimmy Connors 6–1, 6–1, 4–1 in the fourth round. Indeed, so certain was *The Times* of the outcome that, unknown to their then tennis correspondent, the peerless Rex Bellamy, they published a first edition carrying news of four Swedes – Edberg, Wilander, Anders Jarryd and Pernfors – qualifying for the quarter-finals of the Wimbledon men's singles. To the acute embarrassment of that august organ, from the very jaws of victory, Pernfors contrived to snatch an unlikely defeat 6–1, 6–1, 5–7, 4–6, 2–6. It was, as he so succinctly put it, 'a bloody nightmare'.

Another nightmare awaited him in Memphis where Agassi gave the first public showing of his unquestioned genius – and his new-found bonhomie. He applauded his opponent's good shots, clowned around good-naturedly with the line judges and, when Pernfors berated himself in sing-song Swedish, replied: 'That's easy for you to say, Mikael.' After clinching the title with a trusty double-fisted backhand winner, a jubilant Agassi ran over to hug Mike, Betty and Phil sitting in a line in the front row, and donated his racquet as a memento to a young fan in a wheelchair. Even if it was premeditated, it was a master-stroke of public relations and Agassi featured prominently on the next day's news bulletins and newspaper pages. A new American hero had been born.

But it was his next two tournament victories which convinced any remaining doubters that this blond tornado was about to hit tennis.

On 1 May Agassi won the prestigious US Clay Court Championship at Charleston, ending Jimmy Arias's latest comeback in the final, and, just seven days later, added the Tournament of Champions title at Forest Hills, where he tamed the furious serving power of Slobodan Zivojinovic, who was born in Belgrade but was by then a Monte Carlo resident. Though Bobo, as he is better known on the circuit, never quite fulfilled the promise of his early years, he was a redoubtable competitor in 1988 when he hovered just outside the top twenty in the world rankings under the guidance of Ion Tiriac, the wily mentor to Boris Becker.

In the summer of 1986 Zivojinovic had come agonisingly close to beating Ivan Lendl in a thrilling five-set Wimbledon semi-final, and was still a potent enough force two years later when he served for victory against Mats Wilander in the French Open in Paris a fortnight after losing to Agassi at Forest Hills. Wilander regained the initiative and went on to win his third Roland Garros title, while Zivojinovic went into a decline from which he has yet to recover.

And so it was that when Agassi flew into Rome's Leonardo da Vinci airport from New York to prepare for the 1988 Italian Open, he found himself already elevated to superstar status at the Foro Italico, where the young fashion-conscious Italian tennis fans are forever on the lookout for a glamorous new hero, even if he did have to share top billing with Argentine pin-up Gabriela Sabatini. There was a time when Roman manhood would rather be caught eating a plate of alphabet spaghetti, or riding a moped while wearing a crash-helmet, or even making a spritzer with his flagon of Frascati, than watch a women's tennis match. Real macho men do not like women's tennis, so even the greats – Billie Jean King, Chris Evert and Martina Navratilova – were ignored, doomed to play before an empty stadium at nine o'clock in the morning before the serious action (the men) began at 2 p.m.

La Sabatini changed all that (ever since Cleopatra the Romans have been suckers for brunettes with smouldering dark eyes) and even her 9 p.m. practice sessions held under the floodlights of the Foro Italico drew large, vociferous (and predominantly male) crowds. It has to be said that this had less to do with the quality of Sabatini's heavily whipped backhand than the fact she invariably wore the shortest shorts in all Rome.

When the men's championship began and Agassi finally emerged, it seemed as though every beautiful signora and signorita between the ages of fifteen and fifty had turned out to watch, and his progress through the various rounds was greeted with scenes of ecstatic approval.

It must be stressed that the Italian Championship, which began in 1930, is one of the truly great titles in tennis, standing right at the very top of the second tier of tournaments, just underneath the four main events – Wimbledon, the French, Australian and US Opens – which comprise the historic Grand Slam. The list of past winners is proof of the Foro's royal lineage, containing the names of Tilden (1930), Drobny (1950, 1951, 1953), Hoad (1956), Pietrangeli (1957, 1961), Laver (1962, 1971), Newcombe (1969), Nastase (1970, 1973), Borg (1974, 1978), Panatta (1976), Lendl (1986) and Wilander (1987). The spectators who annually flock to the Campo Centrale remain the most passionate and heated in world tennis.

Without an Italian champion of their own since the great days of Adriano Panatta, the noble citizens of the Foro Italico are happy to 'adopt' any visitor who 'plays in the Italian spirit'. Nastase was an ever-popular presence, as were the Spanish Manuels, Santana and Orantes, Frenchmen Yannick Noah and

Henri Leconte, Mecir and, of course, McEnroe. The coldly pragmatic Borg was never warmly received (even before he had the temerity to defeat their beloved Panatta), nor was Lendl, whose grim aspect, facial contortions and physical twitches were always the cause of much ribald laughter. A huffy Steffi Graf never returned to defend the women's singles championship she won in 1987 after one Italian newspaper made mention of her 'Roman' nose.

Agassi, exciting, flamboyant, dashing and daring, was, not unnaturally, immediately adored.

'He is,' said Nastase in 1988 after watching the American lose an exciting semi-final to Argentine Guillermo Perez-Roldan, who suffered defeat the following afternoon in a tense five-set final against Lendl, 'quite, quite brilliant. I can't believe how hard he hits the ball. It's like he's carrying a gun. No one hit like that in my day. Listen to me, Tiriac didn't drive that fast. It is very early in his career, but yes, he could be exactly what tennis has been searching for. The crowds, especially the younger ones, obviously love him.

'He's not an artist, like a Manuel Santana or a Nicola Pietrangeli, but he is not boring to watch, the exact opposite in fact, because although he is a baseliner by instinct, he can do many things and play in many styles, believe me. Better than Borg? As a champion no, not yet, and maybe never. Borg won so many titles. But as a spectacle, then I would have to say yes. Agassi is better to watch. Is good to have someone with sex appeal back in tennis, I think. Is good to have someone who takes risks. Everyone is so serious all of the time these days. If the people behind him are smart, Agassi is going to be very big, maybe the biggest ever. Laver, McEnroe, even me, we were never making videos or posters or having our tennis clothes specially designed.

'Tennis is changing, maybe some think not for the better but who is to say? It will become less of a sport in the future and more of an entertainment. But that is not necessarily a bad thing.

All sports, I think, will become more aware of their image. But the players must know they have to change also. They are not just athletes any more, they must be entertainers.'

Five years on, the Romanian is delighted to have been proved correct and was an avid spectator at Wimbledon last July when the Las Vegan laid claim to the one great title denied the one-time wild man from Transylvania. 'Sure, I believe it's good for tennis. He has magic. I know some people want him to alter his personality, but why? They wanted me to change, but I never hear them, eh?' Twenty-one summers since his heroic Centre Court defeat against Stan Smith in the 1972 Wimbledon final, Nastase still attracts an audience wherever he roams. At forty-seven, the hair remains unfashionably long and lank with the merest hint of grey flecks, the baggy Armani jacket cannot quite camouflage the spreading waistline, and a double chin now sits atop the Gucci silk tie. But the charisma survives, and few in tennis talk with more feeling or intelligence.

'Everybody say if I hadn't done this, if I hadn't done that, I would have won more championships. I know most people think that, but I don't think so. You can't say if I behave differently I'd be a better player. Borg did it his way, and I did it mine. That's how I win matches – and that's how I lose. Same with Agassi. He'll win championships and he'll lose them. Change his personality, his character, then you will change him.'

Though Nastase admits he would 'love to play Agassi just one time', he has no regrets, despite twice finishing runner-up at Wimbledon, to Smith in 1972 and to Borg four years later. 'Of course it would be nice to turn the clock back, maybe for just one day. Sure, I envied Agassi his moment with the trophy, but no, I am not haunted by the memory of those defeats. I do not believe I am going to lie awake at night for the rest of my life because I don't win Wimbledon. When you lose 7–5 in the fifth set as I did it's a disappointment, but I lost that Wimbledon final to Smith because of one or two points, that's all. Same story Ivanisevic. One or two points the other way he is Wimbledon champion and Agassi is the loser. One or two points, what does that mean in a lifetime?

'Agassi is a lot like me in some ways. I was never a machine like Borg, like Lendl. If winning was everything to me then I wouldn't have been as I was on court. I wouldn't be a lunatic, always talking to a linesman, or another person in the stands. I'd like to have been winning all the time – as I'm sure Agassi would – but with my personality and the way I like to play tennis, I couldn't do it.'

Back in that May of 1988, however, another major championship loomed far larger than Wimbledon on Agassi's immediate horizon.

It is not only the band of clay court specialists from South America and Europe who carve out a living on the terracotta circuit who rate the French Open as the very best of the four Grand Slams; many of the leading players, umpires and officials regard Roland Garros, nestling among the horse chestnuts in the Bois de Boulogne, as providing the finest organisation, atmosphere and spectacle, contrasting unfavourably, and then only very slightly, with Wimbledon only in terms of history and tradition. The All England Club dates back to 1922, and before then the championships were played on the other side of Wimbledon Village in the Worple Road grounds which opened in 1877, whilst Roland Garros was constructed in 1928.

It was originally built to host the Davis Cup final of that year, when the legendary Four French Musketeers – Toto Brugnon, Rene Lacoste, Henri Cochet and Jean Borotra – defended the trophy they had prised from the Americans twelve months earlier in Philadelphia. An area of land belonging to the Stade Français tennis club on the edge of the Bois near Porte d'Auteuil was purchased, the only proviso being that the new stadium be named after one of the club's most illustrious members, Roland Garros, a World War I French air force fighter pilot who had been shot down and killed in aerial combat just five weeks before the Armistice in October 1918. Curiously, the air ace was renowned more for his hockey and rugby playing exploits than his expertise with a tennis racquet.

Though the complex spreads yearly under the tender stewardship of French Tennis Federation president Philippe Chatrier, Roland Garros has been modernised sympathetically, its very 'Frenchness' emphasised by the view from the magnificent centre court of the Eiffel Tower peeking out above the dense woods. Roland Garros has always displayed a style all of its own. Torben Ulrich, the Danish beatnik who played jazz clarinet in a St Germain cellar club by night and teasing drop shots by day in the swinging 1960s, used to pedal to the courts on a ramshackle old bike, racquets tied to his back by a length of grubby string and often with a beautiful young mademoiselle in tow. Andre Agassi and his contemporaries, by contrast, sweep up to the front gates in chauffeur-driven limousines. But Chatrier has steadfastly refused to allow much else to change.

The Four Musketeers are immortalised in bronze, their statues standing by a plashing fountain in the cobbled courtyard under the giant scoreboards. The main entrance is named after France's queen of tennis, Suzanne Lenglen, and the spectators are an interesting mix of celebrities such as the film star Gerard Depardieu, stunning film starlets, and large families who combine a day's sport with some serious picnicking. Tennis being a sport of the proletariat in France, you need not be rich, famous or even 'in the know' to acquire tickets for at least one day out of the fortnight, and it is common to see a family group enjoying a hearty lunch of baguettes, cheese, ham, pâté and fruit all washed down with a flask or three of chilled Beaujolais before weaving their way to the centre court.

Invariably, the combination of heavy wine and early summer sun leaves the Roland Garros masses in wildly enthusiastic mood; poor shots which Dan Maskell might have euphemistically described as 'a shade unfortunate' are derisively booed, the arrival of every remotely attractive woman spectator is greeted with a cacophony of wolf whistling, during which play is stopped, and local heroes like Henri Leconte are treated to the Parisian version of the Wembley roar for any excuse.

Glamour abounds where'er your eye wanders. Yves Saint Laurent may have been telling the women of Paris to lower their hemlines for the past two years, but the *mini-jupe* grows ever shorter at Roland Garros where the longest skirts are invariably those adorning the legs of the female tennis players. The umpires are dressed in fashionably crushed linen outfits designed by Hugo Boss, the ball boys and girls by Le Coq Sportif, and the elegant hostesses who show you to your seat in the grandstands by Lacoste. It has long been a (male) tradition of the French tennis championships to spot the single most gorgeous woman of the entire tournament. A few years back the winner was a statuesque Parisienne model who strolled around in a downpour wearing nothing but a completely see-through plastic raincoat.

It was Nastase (who else?) who once observed: 'If you don't like what you see at Roland Garros, you're too old to be looking.'

But back to the tennis. There are two breeds of foreign men's singles champions in Paris. Most, like Borg and Lendl, are respected for their athleticism and determination, but a precious few, such as Panatta, Nastase and Rosewall, are remembered with the same affection bestowed upon any of the great French heroes of the past: Lacoste, Borotra, Cochet, Marcel Barnard and Yannick Noah, the last home winner in 1983. To the wonderfully enthusiastic crowds who flock to Roland Garros each May, it is never enough simply to win, every victory should be a triumph of style, of passion, of flair, one reason why the arrival of Agassi at Roland Garros in 1988 caused such a frisson of excitement.

The three ways to play on the slow clay of Paris are (a) to adopt the 'Stefan Edberg method' and stubbornly ignore its characteristics by persevering with one's natural serve-volley approach, (b) follow the 'mad dogs and Englishmen' gospel of Borg and Lendl and stay out in the midday sun until your opponent crumbles through sunstroke, mental exhaustion or sheer boredom, and (c) as a graduate of the Roland Garros Academy for the Performing Arts, play with grace and artistry. Agassi, almost uniquely, was regarded as being someone who could adapt to any style he chose depending on the particular circumstances.

Those reared solely on television pictures of Wimbledon would be astounded by Roland Garros. At its best, clay court tennis is the stuff of dreams, of Nastase conjuring an outrageous backhand winner, of Santana throwing up a lob so heavily disguised it might have come down wearing dark glasses and a false moustache, of a Pietrangeli drop shot landing as gently as a feather in the breeze; at its worst, the Lendl–Wilander French Open final of 1987, for instance, it is for the eyes of masochists only. Even six years on, that grim affair, which began in daylight and ended some five hours later in pitch darkness and pouring rain, remains painfully fixed in the memory. As the rallies went on, and on, and on, often beyond a hundred strokes, the jokes came thick and fast: 'It's the first time I've ever seen the stewards throwing people IN'; 'Never mind the balls, change the players'; 'Do you see that linesman with the long white beard? Well, he was clean-shaven at the start of this match.' The winner of the English section, courtesy of Derek Parr, the then Reuters sports correspondent in Paris, was: *'Bourez cela pour un jeu de soldats!'* which, roughly speaking, means: 'Sod this for a game of soldiers!'

But there was to be nothing soporific about Agassi's play at Roland Garros that May as he stormed past the rising Swede Magnus Gustafsson in the fourth round, and then slaughtered Perez-Roldan, his conqueror in Rome two weeks earlier and the French Open junior champion of 1986 and 1987, in straight sets in the quarter-finals. But between him and the final stood the intimidating presence of Mats Wilander, champion in 1982, runner-up in 1983, champion for a second time in 1985 and losing finalist to Lendl in that dreadful climax to the 1987 championship.

Wilander was, in fact, the first player to give Swedish tennis a good name. Once dubbed 'more boring than Borg', by 1988, when he was still but twenty-three, he had also won three Australian Open titles and emerged as a thoroughly engaging man both on and off the court, a remarkable transformation for a player who, when he completed his first French Open triumph, had been greeted as a Borg clone, a dour baseliner who was even more difficult to watch than he was to beat. But the Wilander awaiting Agassi was by now a very different athlete, a more adventurous player who had won his five Grand Slam titles on three different surfaces – French clay and Australian grass and hard courts – a feat which had always proved beyond his illustrious fellow-Swede.

In the event, the eagerly awaited duel between Wilander and Agassi on the centre court at Roland Garros was a minor classic, the twice champion edging home 4–6, 6–2, 7–5, 5–7, 6–0. Wilander's recollection of that day is of a titanic struggle until Agassi finally wilted in the fifth and final set. 'It was one of my hardest matches at Roland Garros that year, or any other for that matter,' says the Swede. 'For four sets Andre played classic clay court tennis. He stayed back, he came in, he varied the pace, he used different spins. But no matter how hard he hit the ball, it was always with amazing accuracy. I do remember he hit the lines far more often than you would expect. I guess a few of the guys in the locker room at the time still weren't sure about him, about whether he had the game and the mind to be a champion. If they'd played against him in that semi-final at Roland Garros they might not have had the same doubts.'

Jon-Anders Sjogren, the Swedish Davis Cup coach who guided Wilander to his seven Grand Slam championships and to the world number one ranking he held for a short spell in 1988, was similarly convinced: 'Anyone who could match Mats ball for ball for four sets at his peak has to be a little bit special, I think. We had known it was going to be a tough match, for although Mats was a two-time champion in Paris, Agassi had a remarkable talent and had already proved he was a serious threat on a clay court. Of course, the similarities to Borg were obvious, but he had much more variation than Borg and that is what made him so popular with the crowds.

'When Borg went out to play a tennis match, he went to war. Even four or five years ago it was obvious Agassi viewed the court more as a stage. Mats was a wonderful athlete, however, though he may not have looked it to the inexperienced eye. He covered the court as fast as anyone I ever saw, and he made his opponents work incredibly hard for each point. He always placed the ball exactly where they didn't want it to go. That's why Agassi became so tired. By the start of the fifth set he was mentally and physically exhausted.'

It was during his Paris exertions that Agassi, who had then risen to fifth in the world (two years earlier he had stood at number 230), first revealed he did not intend playing Wimbledon in 1988, a decision which stunned his fellow-professionals and outraged those who believe the entire sport of tennis is constructed around that sacred fortnight in late June and early July. The official reason was 'tiredness', though he proceeded to play for the next four months without a break. 'I don't know why everyone puts so much emphasis on Wimbledon,' said his agent Bill Shelton by way of explanation. 'It's just another tournament like all the rest. It's simply not on Andre's schedule at present and anyway he needs a rest between the clay court and hard court seasons. Andre will play Wimbledon one day. Wimbledon is going to be around.' His gratuitously offensive words were to come back to embarrass him four years later.

Rather than quell the mutterings that he was running scared, the decision and the bizarre reasoning behind it served only to fuel rumours that Agassi's entourage was protecting its employer from another Leconte fiasco. Ivan Lendl, who skipped

Wimbledon in 1982 after losing to Australian Charlie Fancutt ('I made a lot of people famous at Wimbledon in those days'), now admits it was an error of judgement. 'I really thought I couldn't play on grass and that was why I stayed away, but in my heart I knew it was the biggest tournament of them all, and I knew I would have to return some day, the sooner the better. With the benefit of hindsight, I would say Andre had been ill-advised.' Jimmy Connors, never one to hide from an adversary or an unsympathetic court surface, chided: 'That's where you make the name on which everything else hangs.' Even Stefan Edberg, who is seldom known to say an unkind word about anyone, felt forced to pronounce the following judgement: 'It's a little bit sad when the fifth-best player in the world doesn't want to play the number one championship in the world.'

Agassi had made his Davis Cup debut for the Stars and Stripes in the American Zone semi-final tie against Peru in Lima earlier in the year and beaten local hero Jaime Yzaga 6–8, 7–5, 6–1, 6–2 in an arena seething with hostility. In July 1988 he was thrown into another bubbling cauldron of pent-up animosity in Buenos Aires, Argentina, a matter of days after Edberg beat Boris Becker in four sets to win his first Wimbledon title. The United States had to beat Argentina in Buenos Aires to regain their place among the elite nations in the following year's competition after being relegated from the Davis World Group in 1987. They had been humiliated by Paraguay in the white heat of Asuncion, where Ken Flach and Robert Seguso were subjected to death threats, and then by Germany in Connecticut.

Inspired by the feats of Guillermo Vilas, who was ranked in the top ten every year between 1974 and 1982, during which time he won the French, US and two Australian Open titles, Argentina had emerged as a major world power in tennis, especially before their vociferous home crowd in Buenos Aires. Its latest gauchos, Guillermo Perez-Roldan and Martin Jaite, were among the very best in the world, especially on slow clay.

Though Agassi had beaten the cunning Yzaga, he had little

understanding of what might await him in the Argentine capital, while John McEnroe had lost all four previous singles there against Vilas and his regular sidekick Jose-Luis Clerc. 'It would be nice to win this one, because I don't think we've won here in twenty-five years,' McEnroe grinned on arrival. Reminded that the United States had, in fact, never won a Davis Cup tie in Buenos Aires, McEnroe's grin grew even wider. 'Right. I knew it was a long time. Nobody else in America might care about this match, but this is a personal vendetta against Argentina. I want us to win in this stadium.'

And win they did, McEnroe bewitching Perez-Roldan with a vintage display, and Agassi crushing Jaite 6–2, 6–2, 6–1, a victory which had the rest of the American team shaking their heads in disbelief. 'It was amazing,' relives US Davis Cup captain Tom Gorman. 'In that icy wind in Buenos Aires, he warmed up with two or three forehands and backhands and a few serves, then said, "Let's go." Then he routed Jaite.' McEnroe, too, was awed by what he saw. 'Andre's timing, his eye, his ability to pick up the ball, is incredible. His mix of shots, the drops and lobs, the way he wallops that forehand is phenomenal. He's still a kid, but he has that confidence, the attitude, the feeling of a champion. Listen, Lendl made himself a great player, but he was never a natural. The last guy like Agassi was Becker, before him Wilander, before him . . .' The word 'me' was allowed to drift unspoken in the air.

Having snubbed Wimbledon for reasons best known to himself, the one tournament neither the new wonder boy nor his team of advisers had any intention of missing was the US Open to be played at Flushing Meadow during the first fortnight in September. Agassi had lost in the first round in 1986 and 1987, but in 1988 he was being talked about as a possible dark-horse champion. Unlike the two previous years, he was now considerably experienced and was entering the fray in the middle of a rich seam of good form, having won the Mercedes Cup in Stuttgart, the Volvo International at Stratton

Mountain and the Mennen Cup in Illinois, the fourth, fifth and sixth Grand Prix titles of a remarkable season during which he had put together a winning streak of twenty-three matches and become a Davis Cup regular. Only four Americans had won the US championship since tennis went 'open' in 1968, Arthur Ashe, Stan Smith, McEnroe and Connors, and hopes were high that the illustrious quartet would swiftly become a quintet.

The Agassi phenomenon was sweeping the United States where his appeal crossed every social and ethnic boundary. He was as American as apple pie, though he came from poor immigrant stock; to teenage girls he was young and sexy, while his waif-like smile brought out the mothering instinct in an older generation; he was rebellious yet he was a born-again Christian who read the scriptures daily. No wonder all New York wanted to turn out to greet him.

A word about Flushing Meadow. Unlike the French, who built their stadium within earshot of the willow warblers who inhabit the Bois de Boulogne, when the USTA decided to assemble a new National Tennis Center they flung Flushing Meadow on top of an old rubbish tip, quite appropriate considering its appearance. An indescribably ugly concrete monstrosity, it looks not unlike San Quentin prison. In fact some say the only difference is that at Flushing Meadow they do open the gates to let you out at night. Nonetheless, some 40,000 braying New Yorkers make the daily trek from Manhattan across the East River out to the less than royal borough of Queens, either by car (a tortuous journey) or subway (an unnerving experience) to where Flushing Meadow sits in all its gory glory, an ugly claustrophobic mix of heat, smells, jostling crowds, directly under the flight path out of La Guardia Airport but a misdirected forehand away.

Though the US Open traditionally attracts a goodly assortment of celebrities, for example Charlton Heston, Cher, Whitney Houston, Mickey Rourke, Bruce Springsteen, Eddie Murphy, Don Johnson and Melanie Griffith, the typical spectator is overexcited, over fifty, and usually 35 pounds overweight. The fashion at Flushing Meadow is to be seen clothed from head to toe in the most expensive tennis gear around, which is why it is not uncommon to find yourself involuntarily giving up half your seat to a Pavarotti-shaped New York cab driver obscenely squeezed into a pair of skin-tight crimson cycling shorts. Andre Agassi, you have much to answer for. For some unfathomable reason some spectators even carry an armful of racquets.

Tennis is very much a sideshow to the main event at Flushing Meadow, which is sampling as many forms of fast food as is humanly possible in one afternoon; hot dogs dripping mustard, cheeseburgers, pizzas smothered in mozzarella and sun-dried tomatoes, fiery chili, salt beef sandwiches the length of the Lincoln Tunnel, Italian tagliatelli, Mexican tortillas, baked potatoes with every conceivable topping, and ice-cream of every imaginable flavour.

Away from the rowdy queues, the squabbles over squatters' rights at the few tables, the chomping, slurping, belching hordes, lies Flushing Meadow's showpiece, the Stadium Court. Think of the Centre Court at Wimbledon, and now imagine it covered in cheerless concrete painted battleship-grey, filled with 18,000 demented souls and plonked down on the edge of the runway at Heathrow. This is an animal farm. Unlike the spectators at Wimbledon, who sit in dignified silence until their polite applause marks the end of each rally, the average New York tennis fan has an attention span of around thirty seconds. They are thus incapable of watching more than two successive points before standing up in mid-rally, pushing their way to the nearest aisle and shambling off in search of a diet (ha!) coke and a tub of popcorn which comes in three sizes, large, huge and extra-large dustbin.

The stewards, as merry a crew of beer-bellied pirates as you could wish to avoid, serve only to exacerbate matters with their hysterical shouting and gesticulating, while a US Air DC10 thunders by inches overhead and the umpire pleads for calm. It was in the midst of all these goings on – plus a John McEnroe tantrum – that this hellish din was suddenly interrupted during the 1988 US Open by the ringing of Donald Trump's portable phone in one of the VIP boxes at courtside. 'That's La Guardia,' said the man from *The Scotsman*, 'to ask if we can possibly keep the noise down.'

Despite, or maybe because of, the hullabaloo going on all around him, Agassi plotted an uneventful path to the quarter-finals, where, after beating the precocious Michael Chang in straight sets in the fourth round, he was drawn to meet the ageing but deadly dangerous Jimmy Connors in a quarter-final tie to be played at night under Flushing Meadow's floodlights. Flushing Meadow at night can be a scary place where danger lurks in the shadows. The planes may have been grounded for the night, but the sounds of the adjacent railroad echo eerily in the distance, while the mob, their inhibitions freed by bucketfuls of cold beer and the surrounding darkness, hoot and holler like a wrestling crowd. 'They're animals,' grinned Connors, then a sprightly thirty-six, 'and boy, do I love getting in that cage with them. I've played all my best tennis out there at night, unlike a lot of players. Borg, for instance, never got to grips with all this chaos. Me? I thrive on it. Every point, every game, every set is war.'

Connors was a remnant from the days when Stan Smith earned £5,000 for winning the 1972 Wimbledon championship (Agassi would win over £250,000 in 1992), when tennis clothing was not just white but positively snow white, and when racquets were fashioned out of hickory. 'Dealing with age is no big deal,' he said at Flushing Meadow after crushing Mexican number one Jorge Lozano for the loss of just three games in the fourth round. 'I've never believed being thirty-five or thirty-six or whatever is a problem if you've stayed in good shape.'

Connors relishes his image as a battle-scarred old alley cat, and before their quarter-final Battle of the Generations, Bollettieri was at pains to convince Agassi, aged eighteen, that here was an opponent worthy of the greatest respect. His world ranking was just beginning to slip, but no player, before or since, could still spit in the face of Father Time with such defiant contempt. With five US Open titles (1974, 1976, 1978, 1982 and 1983), two Wimbledon (1974, 1982) and one Australian (1974), Agassi was confronting a living legend.

Many young players have cracked against such an opponent, but Agassi thrived on the Stadium Court stage that night, winning 6–2, 7–6, 6–1 with a spellbinding display of muscle power and daring. His only serious mistake came in the after-match press conference when he revealed: 'Actually I told a friend before I went out to play I thought I'd win three, three and three. I really didn't think Jimmy would have that much in him.'

This insensitivity, some called it insolence, could be put down to the sheer exuberance any player of his age feels in the immediate aftermath of such a famous victory, but, to the sceptics, it was further evidence that Agassi's well-polished boy-next-door image was obscuring an altogether less ingenuous character. By New Year's Eve 1988, he had risen to number three on the ATP computer rankings, had banked over $2 million in prize money and endorsements and was generally regarded as a champion-in-waiting – but one who had made as many enemies as friends. The first signs of any fall, almost inevitable given the speed and height of his rise, was awaited with more than a hint of impatience by some.

5

The Fall of a Rebel

Andre Agassi brought more to tennis than a deadly backhand, Bon Jovi hair-do and a strikingly colourful appearance. He made great play of applauding his opponents' winning returns in the most ostentatious manner, though usually only when he was well on the way to victory. He greeted his own good shots with a schoolboy cheer, liked to reward any applause from the gallery with a theatrical bow, would pretend to bribe line judges to change any particularly close calls in his favour, would blow kisses or throw shirts, balls, sweatbands and assorted souvenirs into the crowd, and, when it began to rain, would borrow an umbrella and make as if to continue playing. To the adoring teenyboppers he was 'a real cutie', to his highly professional marketing machine he was Mr Charisma, and to the cynics, he became the 'Great White Hype', the 'Sham of Persia', the 'Bland Bombshell', or, most memorable of all, 'Scumbagassi'. But 'I'm just trying to enjoy myself out there so everyone else can enjoy me,' he pleaded innocently.

Ion Tiriac, however, who had become a living legend in the art of gamesmanship during his playing days alongside Ilie Nastase in the Romanian Davis Cup team, but who is now admired as one of the least duplicitous personalities in tennis, warned: 'God help Agassi if and when he starts losing. It may be all right to prance around like an idiot when you're on top, but what seems funny now will not appear quite so amusing when the winning stops.' McEnroe, who would later succeed in persuading Agassi to moderate, if not entirely eradicate, the patronising applause bestowed upon his rivals, concurred: 'That sort of thing is just rubbing other people's faces in it. Players don't like that kind of thing. Hopefully, he'll grow out of it.'

Though the triumphal headlines of 1988 had helped divert attention away from his antics, there had been a growing sense of unease among the players at his 'showboating' (American phraseology for blatant exhibitionism). And when the new season began in January with yet another highly publicised boycott – this time of the Australian Open at Flinders Park, Melbourne – the whispers grew ever louder.

Apart from the Connors gaff at the US Open the previous September, Agassi had shocked decent tennis society during his unquestionably superb Davis Cup victory over Argentine Martin Jaite in Buenos Aires. He deliberately humiliated an obviously beaten and dejected opponent. Leading 6–2, 6–2, 4–0, but trailing 0–40, an indefensibly insensitive Agassi loudly shouted over to Bollettieri at courtside: 'Hey, Nick, watch this.' He then caught Jaite's next serve in his left hand like a cricketer, thereby conceding the point to Jaite as if to say, 'Since you can't win by your own efforts, here, have this game on me.' The outraged Argentines in the Buenos Aires Lawn Tennis Club (nary a blade of grass in sight) whistled their disapproval at such a display of superciliousness, a sentiment echoed by McEnroe, who, for all his excesses, has never deliberately humbled the man on the other side of the net: 'Andre was young and naive back then, but what he did was unbelievable. Too much ham, and too insulting to the other guy.'

Though he foolishly attempted to explain away the inexplicable at the time by admitting in all seriousness: 'It was just something I've always wanted to do,' Agassi now sounds suitably contrite: 'If I could go back in time, then obviously I wouldn't have done it. I never wanted to demean Martin Jaite, no way. Especially since he's one of the nicest guys on the tour.'

Emboldened by the chorus of disapproval which greeted his antics in Argentina, Agassi's critics spoke with increasing candour and by now countless other tales of past misdemeanours were beginning to surface, including a whole litany of peccadilloes from the 1988 Volvo Cup at Los Angeles where he first provided evidence that he would deliberately 'tank' (lose) a set in order to conserve energy for later in the match, one of the most heinous 'crimes' in professional tennis. Agassi worked the ruse against Mexico's Jorge Lozano in the first round, and repeated the manoeuvre in an untidy 6–4, 0–6, 6–4 defeat of McEnroe in an ill-tempered semi-final. 'It's insulting, immature and a cop-out,' fumed McEnroe. 'Agassi's act is beginning to wear thin. I don't believe that's showing respect for yourself or your opponent. And it's not good for tennis either. I expect we'll see a lot more of this kind of thing.'

Later beaten by Mikael Pernfors in the final, Agassi accepted the sizeable runners-up cheque before delivering the most ungracious of speeches, dismissing his unexpected defeat by way of a number of imaginative excuses before turning his wrath on one particular spectator who had been vocal in his support of the Swede calling him a 'jerk'. But the *pièce de résistance* of Agassi's shameful week in Los Angeles had occurred in his quarter-final against mild-mannered Australian Mark Woodforde, who was politely pleading his case in a disputed line call debate with the umpire when a voice from the other side of the court intervened: 'Hey, why don'tcha leave the guy alone, he's only trying to do his job.' When an opponent is arguing with an official, it is common courtesy for a professional tennis player to keep his own counsel; he should never, ever, become embroiled in the contretemps himself, no matter how tempted. Thankfully, the urbane Woodforde, as courteous as he is popular on the circuit, was prepared to give his teenage taunter the benefit of the doubt: 'Back then, Andre was a little bit of a – how can I put this nicely? – well, let's just say an upstart. But he's settled down a lot now and even gone out of his way to fit in on the tour. Now when we see each other we always chat, there are certainly no hard feelings.'

Having chosen to pass up the opportunity of making further mischief at the Australian Open in early January, Agassi was quickly into his stride in 1989 when the team from Paraguay, who had still not been forgiven by the United States for that Davis Cup indignity in Asuncion two years before, arrived in Fort Myers, Florida, for a first-round match that was viewed as an exercise in revenge in some quarters. Hugo Chapacu, a Paraguayan hero in 1987, was being routed 6–2, 6–1, 6–1 when Agassi, for reasons known only to himself, began taunting his rival. His explanation? 'It was time to rub it in. But I wasn't making fun of him, I was making fun of Paraguay.' 'Oh,' said a Paraguayan diplomat with heavy irony, 'I guess that's supposed to make it all right, then.'

At this time Agassi was financially on a roll , though he was not playing with quite the same vigour he had displayed before his lengthy Christmas and New Year vacation in Las Vegas. After publicly throwing away the trusty Prince racquet he had wielded since he was a tiny tot, Agassi signed a £4 million, five-year deal with the Belgian manufacturer Donnay, who had been without a top-of-the-bill name since Borg disappeared. Owned by Bernard Tapie, the high-profile French television mogul and president of Marseille football club, Donnay promised and duly manufactured a selection of racquets in every colour of the rainbow. There was one small problem. Having grown up with a Prince in his hand, Agassi was helpless with his fluorescent pink Donnay in his hand.

'I can't serve with this damn thing,' he wailed during the US Professional Indoor Championships in Philadelphia at the end of February when, as Tiriac had forecast, the losing started.

At the Newsweek Champions' Cup in Indian Wells, California (incidentally, this was the last title won by the incomparable Miloslav Mecir), Agassi appeared with what looked suspiciously like his favourite old Prince model with a large 'D' representing Donnay painted on the strings. His agent Bill Shelton decided to take the querulous ladies and gentlemen of the Press into his confidence. 'It was,' he disclosed with due gravitas, 'not a Prince but a Donnay prototype.' Sportingly, Prince ignored this chicanery. Agassi duly became expert with the new Belgian product, and replica models of every hue can now be seen in public parks from Banff to Bodmin.

It was also in Indian Wells that Agassi worked the Californian audience into such a frenzy that he felt obliged to grab the umpire's microphone and, addressing the spectators, offer up a 'heart-felt' plea for calm and impartiality. Outraged by this glaring act of manipulation, his opponent, American Davis Cup veteran Robert Seguso, protested with such vehemence that it was he who was ultimately disqualified and thrown out of the tournament. In the following round Agassi took the microphone again, this time after umpire Jim Zimmerman had overruled a line judge's call and awarded the American an important point at a crucial stage of his match with Yannick Noah. Agassi humbly said the linesman was correct and he therefore could not accept the point. It should go to his French opponent.

Noah looked suitably abashed, some of the audience applauded, but others saw Agassi's apparent munificence as yet another attempt to polish his carefully fostered, squeaky-clean halo.

But that halo was already displaying signs of tarnish. At the Volvo Indoor event at Memphis, which had been the first of his six titles in 1988, Agassi, having dumped the racquet he had carried since childhood, now ditched Wendy Stewart for Amy Moss, a statuesque Tennessee blonde who was working as a courtesy driver for the players during a week's holiday from university. A devout Christian, she would be a permanent presence at Agassi's side for the next two years. Wendy packed her bags and returned to Las Vegas to wait. 'She was hurt, crushed, devastated,' explains a mutual friend, 'but deep down she wasn't worried. She'd known Andre since about the age of seven, so although Amy had simply blown her away, Wendy was content to bide her time. Amy was everything Wendy isn't. She always dressed and acted like a celebrity, and she loved nightclubs and late-night parties. Wendy hates that sort of thing.

'It was as if Wendy knew in her heart that she and Andre were destined to get together again. So she drifted quietly into the background and bided her time. Sure enough, two years later, in the spring of 1991, Andre was back and now they're more in love than ever. All their friends think Wendy is absolutely perfect for Andre. She's low key, in fact so low key you'd hardly notice she's there at times. There was a big change in Andre after the Amy episode. He became quieter, more thoughtful, less outrageous. As anyone who knows her will tell you, that was all Wendy's doing.' Wendy's father, Manny, was delighted to see them reunited: 'She helps keep Andre's life in order. She packs his cases before they set off for every tournament, she sorts out and replies to all his fan letters, she can put a grip on his racquet handle and is even learning how to do a restring. For Wendy, it's the very reason for her existence. She's always there for Andre, it's that simple.'

During the early days of her absence in 1989, Agassi's reputation plummeted; he was variously accused of avoiding tournaments containing other top-ten players, of continued 'tanking', of feigning injury to excuse a number of mysterious withdrawals, of cynically using his born again Christianity as a marketing ploy, of putting the rush to become a multi-millionaire before the grind of becoming a champion, of hiding behind his faintly absurd entourage and of selling himself to the highest bidder.

To a lesser degree, all the leading players travel with a

support group of friends, relations and coaches. Ivan Lendl, for instance, will be accompanied by his wife Samantha, three young daughters, Marika and the twins Caroline and Isabelle, and long-time mentor Tony Roche at all the major championships. Some groups have names. There is Team Capriati, Monica's Masses, the Chang Gang, Martina's Mob and so on. However, it was Andre Agassi who first turned the 'entourage' into an art form. The personnel change from time to time, though the numbers usually remain constant. In its original form it consisted of Nick Bollettieri (Korean War veteran turned suntanned tennis guru), brother Phil Agassi (counsellor and chief bag carrier), Gil Reyes (physical fitness overseer and 'certainly not a bodyguard, whatever you might think'), agent Bill Shelton (a.k.a. Dr No for his idiosyncratic way of not helping the media), Fritz Glauss (travelling church minister), the ever-loyal Wendy Stewart, plus an assorted posse of attendants from Donnay and Nike. With their matching dark glasses, elaborate clothes and glowing good health they resemble a family pop group. The rhyming properties of Gil, Phil and Bill immediately caused them to be dubbed the Three Stooges.

Despite this planeload of advisers, flatterers, trainers, amateur psychologists, managers, sparring partners, spokesmen and highly paid porters, Agassi, or Andre the Client as he had become known owing to the vast number of advertising deals he was involved in, was surprisingly unprepared when he did manage to squeeze in the occasional game of tennis betwixt his dizzying round of business deals. At the important Lipton International Players' Championship in Key Biscayne, Florida, which rates just one notch below Grand Slam status, he suffered a stunning first-round defeat against Carl-Uwe Steeb, then boasted he had never heard of his conqueror before that day and had not realised he played left-handed until they had started knocking-up. 'Charlie' Steeb had, in fact, represented what was then West Germany at the inaugural tennis tournament in the 1988 Seoul Olynpics and would finish 1989 ranked fifteenth in the world. How could Agassi and Gil, Phil and Bill not know he was a left-hander?

In the spring of 1989, Agassi, a six-times winner on the Grand Prix tour in 1988 and twice losing finalist, was gradually sliding down the rankings. Another day, another unexpected defeat, this time to David Wheaton, and he stormed off court barking out his latest petulant order to Nick Bollettieri: 'Fire Fritz.'

He went to the Italian Open in Rome, where for once he allowed himself to be tempted away from McDonald's in the Via Nazionale to sample the famous pasta dishes at Sabatini's (no relation), one of the world's most romantic restaurants tucked away in an idyllic courtyard off the Piazza Santa Maria and set against a backdrop of fountains and twelfth-century church belltower. Being in the Eternal City and playing before the manic multitudes of the Foro Italico briefly inspired Agassi, who had recently celebrated his nineteenth birthday. He surged into the final, where, as was to become a disturbingly frequent occurrence, he surrendered from a strong position, losing 3–6, 6–4, 6–2, 6–7, 1–6 to the new Argentine heart-throb Alberto Mancini ('pronounced gorgeous' wrote Sue Mott in the *Sunday Times*), whose great-grandfather had been born in southern Italy.

Though he was undeniably immensely popular and had played his best tennis in over six months, Agassi was extremely sour in defeat and launched his post-match press conference by shouting to brother Phil (his ill-fitting toupee had gained the soubriquet of the 'Persian Rug') who was standing guard over his shoulder-bags at the door of the interview room: 'Hey, Phil, you wanna bring those bags up here where I can see them. I wouldn't like anything to go missing.' The assembled newspaper and radio reporters, who had travelled from all over the globe to gather around him that Sunday afternoon, found this a less than Christian attitude.

This surly attitude was all the more difficult to understand because Agassi had come close to beating an opponent who was in the middle of a 'dream sequence'. Mancini, ranked 46 places below the American at the end of 1988, was enjoying a surge which would take him high into the top ten in the world and had recently won the Monte Carlo Open after disposing of Mats Wilander and Boris Becker, ranked second and third on the computer, in successive matches. So impressive had the twenty-year-old Argentine looked that many wise observers believed he could now go on and win the French Open at Roland Garros, thereby completing the elusive 'European clay court grand slam' of Monte Carlo, Rome and Paris, a feat last achieved by Ilie Nastase sixteen years earlier in the spring of 1973 and one which had proved beyond Bjorn Borg, Ivan Lendl and Manuel Santana among others.

In the event Mancini proved unequal to the quest, for he was thrashed in Paris 6–1, 6–3, 7–6 by a peerless Stefan Edberg in a one-sided quarter-final. Agassi went out in four bitter sets to Jim Courier in the third round. He was further humiliated when Michael Chang gained an epic victory over the gallant Edberg in a fluctuating five-set final. The Stars and Stripes flew over Roland Garros in June 1989 for the first time since Tony Trabert's triumph thirty-four years earlier in 1955.

Aged seventeen, seeded fourteen and with a serve no more intimidating than that of Jennifer Capriati, Chang was living proof that, as the French revolutionary Voltaire wrote in 1769, 'God is on the side, not of the heavy battalions, but of the best shots.' Exactly two hundred years after the mob had marched on the Bastille and Marie Antoinette made her unfortunate remark about cake, the Chinese-American served the ruling aristocracy of men's tennis, champion Ivan Lendl and Stefan Edberg, humble pie and became the youngest-ever man to win a Grand Slam championship.

His famous five-hour, 4–6, 4–6, 6–3, 6–3, 6–3 defeat of Lendl in the fourth round was nothing compared to the struggle he had to win over the French spectators. Repeated references to the help he invoked from the Almighty led cynical Parisians to dub his appearances on court 'the God Slot', and his image as a latterday Billy Graham in a Reebok shirt received further gloss when his doting mother, Betty Chang, revealed to anyone who would listen that her son played tennis with the sole purpose of 'spreading the Word'. An active Christian, Chang had immediately thanked 'the Lord Jesus Christ for my victory'.

Lendl gradually became disorientated by the young American's under-arm serve, the teenager's inability to move at anything faster than a hobble due to apparent leg cramp and his disconcerting ability to mix spin, pace and angles. Earlier, with Lendl two sets to the good and in seemingly imperious form, the good citizens of Paris had streamed out of Roland Garros for the traditional 'afternoon tea' of Chablis and Brie. When they returned some time later, their contented mien quickly turned to one of puzzlement as they watched the world's number one, all muscle and sinew, being systematically dismantled by this strip of a lad from Hoboken, New Jersey.

'I prayed and my cramp went away,' Chang revealed. 'You may say there are more important things to pray for, but everything that happens in my life is because of Him. I get my strength from Him, He controls my every action.' After another 4½-hour marathon session against Edberg in the final, Chang also disclosed how his mother's Chinese noodles had helped build up his physical stamina, whilst his mental strength came from a divine source. A few bored boos rang out around the centre court but Chang, who mentioned just about everyone he knew in his victory speech except Edberg at his side, stood his ground just as he had done against Lendl: 'I know every time I bring up the Lord Jesus' name everybody nods. I know you're becoming sick of it, but it's the truth, He gets all the credit.'

With Wimbledon approaching, Agassi, just as he had done twelve months earlier, inexplicably took his annual sabbatical, flying home to Las Vegas ('I need to put on a bit of weight, I don't think I'm physically strong enough to play on grass') while the rest of the tennis circus set up camp at the All

England Club. And again Agassi was the real loser, his absence scarcely noticed by the vast crowds as Becker climaxed another fascinating championship by polishing off Edberg in the final to win his third men's singles crown. Too tired to play in 1988, too frail to cope with grass in 1989, many of his fellow pros were rapidly losing patience with this misguided young man. Although he was now into his third summer as a full-time member of the tour and flaunted all the familiar trappings of celebrity status, he had not as yet deigned to play in two of the four Grand Slam championships, Wimbledon and the Australian Open.

Many believed Agassi was simply running scared, determinedly and artificially boosting his world ranking by avoiding the other leading players whenever possible. The Agassi camp breezily dismissed these suggestions, but although they were correct in claiming some of the sniping was due to sheer jealousy, they were never able to mount a credible argument against the charge that he had attained a world ranking of number three without ever stepping on court against seven of those other men ranked alongside him in the top ten.

Then, just as had happened in Rome after a miserable spring, Agassi found renewed enthusiasm and determination, this time in front of his adoring American public at the 1989 US Open in September. He again reached the quarter-finals, and for the second successive year had to confront Jimmy Connors, now thirty-seven. The score was 6–1, 4–6, 0–6, 6–3, 6–4. This was the first time in his chequered career that Agassi had ever managed to win a five-set brawl, and one of his retinue later let it be known that his super-confident boss had deliberately capitulated in the third set with the sole purpose of ending his unhappy record in marathon matches. Connors was suitably disgusted at this suggestion, which was crass in both its reasoning and presumption.

Having upset one of the great elder statesmen of tennis, Agassi then left McEnroe stuttering with apoplectic rage in Dallas during the WCT Finals when he quit when he was trailing 0–3 in the second set after winning the first. His excuse was an aggravated pulled muscle but the Texan crowd was unimpressed and he limped (for the first discernible time that night) off court with the sound of loud booing in his ears. 'It was,' says one seasoned professional, 'a disgraceful act of surrender.'

Only in the Davis Cup against France did Agassi fully resemble a top-ten player in style and commitment. He inspired a 5–0 whitewash of the visiting French team in a second-round match played in San Diego, California, with a dynamic 6–1, 6–2, 6–7, 6–1 victory against Henri Leconte (revenge for the Wimbledon fiasco of two years before) in a crucial opening singles. Agassi later despatched Yannick Noah in straight sets to record his seventh successive win in Davis Cup singles, a superb record in a competition which has a rich history of Goliaths being unceremoniously tripped up by puny Davids. Now the semi-final draw paired the United States against holders West Germany in the Olympiahalle, Munich, a confrontation which would see the very best and the very worst of Andre Agassi.

The Americans were severely weakened by the late withdrawal of John McEnroe through injury, but they won the opening singles thanks to a tenacious display from the pugnacious substitute Brad Gilbert, who came from behind to subdue Carl-Uwe Steeb 6–2, 2–6, 2–6, 6–4, 6–4. Then Agassi and the German hero Boris Becker combined to produce one of the most tension-packed matches of the entire year. The Las Vegan, making the absolute minimum of mistakes, won the first two sets on tie-breaks and stood but one game away from a momentous triumph at 7–6, 7–6, 6–5. Becker is a hard man to beat, especially in front of a German crowd in the national stadium. He held serve, won the resultant tiebreak, and then claimed the fourth set 6–3 to level the match at two sets all before play was suspended a few minutes past midnight. When the two players returned to the Olympiahalle the following morning, Becker took the final set 6–4 and, less than an hour later, teamed up with Eric Jelen to score a four-set win over the American doubles formation, Ken Flach and Robert Seguso, to leave the West Germans 2–1 in front.

The prospect of a rematch with Steeb, the 'unknown left-hander' who had crushed him in straight sets at the Lipton International Players Championship at Key Biscayne earlier that spring, should have had a galvanising effect on Agassi, who now had to win to square the best-of-five-match semi-final at two rubbers apiece. But Agassi lost 6–4, 4–6, 4–6, 2–6. Worse, he allowed his spirit to be broken and capitulated as soon as he fell behind. As US non-playing captain Tom Gorman strove to inspire his man during each changeover, Agassi could be heard whining despondently: 'It's too tough, it's just too tough.'

He won a tournament title in October 1989 when he defeated his Davis Cup colleague Brad Gilbert to win the Orlando Classic, but the year ended on another disappointing note at the Grand Prix Masters in Madison Square Garden, New York, shortly before Christmas. Agassi was a broken man from the opening night when he lost the first match of his round-robin group 4–6, 2–6 to Stefan Edberg. He then prised just four games off Wimbledon champion Boris Becker and finished with a miserable won 0, lost 3 record by going down 6–3, 3–6, 3–6 to Gilbert. Edberg, beaten by Becker at the group stage, went on to beat his close rival in a four-set final while Agassi went off to spend his year's winnings – $478,901 in official prize money and an estimated $3 million in outside deals – on a Las Vegan Christmas.

The new decade opened with another 'no-show' when Agassi decided to skip the 1990 Australian Open, and he was also missing from the cast list when the United States began their Davis Cup campaign against Mexico in Carslbad, California, in February. There were many, including Tom Gorman, who had grave misgivings about ever calling upon Agassi's services after his abject surrender to Steeb in Munich, but although the American captain was in the unaccustomed position of having seven American players ranked in the world's top ten, injuries to McEnroe, Michael Chang and Aaron Krickstein left him scratching around for a suitable team. Though he was short of match practice, having skipped the Australian Open, Agassi agreed to play – but there was one problem. Gorman demanded that Agassi arrive with a maxiumum of one guest, the rest of his unappreciated entourage was not, repeat not, welcome. A two-hour telephone argument ensued, at the end of which Gorman and Agassi agreed to disagree and Brad Gilbert and Jay Berger were chosen to dispose of a relatively weak Mexican squad.

Perversely, Agassi now chose to return to top form, and won the Volvo Classic in San Francisco, the inaugural event of the new player-controlled ATP Tour. He received two cheques for beating American Todd Witsken in the final, one for the first prize of $30,000 and another for $175,000 in the form of 'appearance money'. There was another big pay-day in March, when he was runner-up to Edberg in the Newsweek Cup at Indian Wells, and then all hell broke loose over the recurring thorny issue of his entourage's right to attend the Davis Cup quarter-final tie against Czechoslovakia in Prague.

After weeks of negotiations and compromise, Agassi agreed to play, joining Brad Gilbert and the new doubles partnership of Rick Leach and Jim Pugh, and the team was duly announced. An hour or so later, Agassi pulled out again, citing an assortment of reasons, the most important of which was Gorman's ban on his entourage, which had been imposed in the hope of building team spirit within the squad. 'I don't see how it's going to help my tennis if I have dinner with Rick Leach and Jim Pugh every night,' explained Agassi huffily. The Davis Cup, one of the most historic competitions in any sport, was being used by one of the most exciting, but infuriating, players in the world as a soapbox from which to air his petty grievances. Even though Agassi had quit the team on two separate occasions, and had been seen to criticise Gorman in print, the real battle was yet to come.

First, however, there was to be triumph, sporting disaster and all sorts of weird and wonderful controversies.

The subject of the next controversy was the Agassi wardrobe as furnished by Nike. As their client's appeal spread, a series of adverts appeared on billboards across the world featuring such slogans as 'The Hair Apparent', 'Just Do It', 'This Will Shake Up The Country Club', and presenting their star attraction resplendent in his new summer collection. The 1990 Agassi was dressed in a variety of colourful creations, such as 'Hot Lava', a tangerine and black ensemble which included denim shorts worn over lurid lurex cycle shorts. Unshaven and long-haired, Agassi took to wearing a single earring and often painted the nail of his little finger in a matching shade. 'Andre Aghastly,' sniffed traditionalists as Agassi swaggered on court looking like a member of a rock band.

Whether it was his clothes, his latest fire-engine-red Donnay, or sheer wilfulness, Agassi now hit a brilliant run of form, culminating in a famous victory in the 128-man Lipton International Players Championship where he thrashed Andres Gomez, Jim Courier and Jay Berger in straight sets before overwhelming a strangely subdued Stefan Edberg in the final.

It was the most important victory of his career to date, against a player who was just about to assume the coveted number one spot on the ATP computer rankings. In a 'sporting' era of pompous, petulant, posturing personalities, Edberg is a throwback to the days of yore; close your eyes and it is easy to picture the Swede in sepia tones, leaping the net to congratulate Perry, Budge or Emerson.

Nor does he cultivate a colourful off-court image. While Agassi, Becker and the others patronise the current 'in' place in London, Paris or Rome, Edberg and his Swedish wife Annette will slip away far from the madding crowd to the nearest pizza parlour. Not surprisingly, Edberg chooses to live in London rather than New York or Monte Carlo because he can eat, shop or practise there in sublime anonymity. 'If you compare

me to Andre or Boris, they're what I would call big stars,'
reflects Edberg modestly. 'They want to be big stars so they
act like they think big stars should act. I'd rather not be known
by anybody.' Though he has been champion of Wimbledon,
Australia and the United States on numerous occasions, Edberg
does not regard himself as a celebrity. 'My life has never really
changed. Why should it? I do the same things I've always done.
Yes, a lot more people recognise me now, especially around
my home in Kensington, but that doesn't really bother me. I
don't make a big deal of it. If you can be natural and be yourself
people aren't going to bother you too much.'

Though one former agent offers the opinion, 'Stefan's polite,
genuine, poised and generous, but he's not exactly scintillating.
It's the likes of Agassi who generate public interest. With Stefan
the reaction tends to be "ho-hum". We talked to him about
his image but he always felt he had to be totally natural.'
A marketing brochure issued by IMG played up this image.
'One might describe Stefan Edberg as a bit of living history.
His approach harks back to the days of the gentleman's game.
The handsome Swede personifies that elusive virtue – class.'

But despite his gentle nature, Edberg has a spine of tungsten
steel to go with his fabulous talent. The Swede's British coach
Tony Pickard says: 'Everyone thinks they have Stefan sussed
out, but they don't. People talk about Jimmy Connors being the
ultimate "street fighter", but they obviously don't know this one.'

Edberg also happens to be one of the most beautiful players
around. Though some glibly dismiss him as a strict serve-
volleyer, that is to ignore the fact that some of his greatest
Davis Cup victories have been achieved on slow red clay. The
frailties of his forehand sometimes let him down, as they did
against Michael Chang in the final of the 1989 French Open at
Roland Garros.

That notorious weakness apart, the Swede is a glorious sight
to behold. He is smooth, effortless, and athletically graceful.
Significantly, the coach who discovered the youngster from

Vastervik always predicted his mental approach would be the key to his future. 'I worked with Edberg until he was nineteen and when he left me I told him he had everything, serve, volley, backhand,' said Percy Rosberg in his little workshop in Bastaad, 'but to be a champion he had to improve his mind. He had to be more aggressive in his head. He had to learn to fight.'

Rosberg played an equally significant role in ensuring that Edberg never developed into a Wilander or Borg clone. 'When he became European junior champion at the age of sixteen, Stefan had a two-fisted backhand just like Borg. I reckoned he should change it and it took him just eight months to be playing the shot with confidence. Now I think it is the best one-handed backhand in the world. It is certainly the most beautiful to watch, though I may be a little bit biased. He's got a very hot fire burning within him. But he's a loner. Everybody likes him but he doesn't let people get too close.'

Though they are too different in their personalities and lifestyles to become close friends, Agassi and Edberg produced a stirring finale to the 1990 Lipton event and the mutual admiration survives to this day. 'I believe Andre is very good for tennis,' says the Swede, 'and not just because he is such a wonderful player. Any sport needs people who look different and act differently from the rest, although, to be honest, I wouldn't choose to wear his clothes. On the other hand it would be pretty boring for everyone if tennis was populated by hordes of Stefan Edbergs.'

The issue of Agassi's ever more garish dress sense took yet another unexpected turn at the start of the 1990 French Open in Paris when the French Tennis Federation chief Philippe Chatrier took a group of British sports writers out to dinner in a tiny bistro far off the tourist track that is frequented by the rugby players of the Racing Club de Paris. Over a memorably delicious pot of cassoulet, Chatrier, under the impression he was speaking off the record, revealed that Agassi's latest outfits might reluctantly persuade him to adopt Wimbledon's 'predominantly white' clothing rule. 'I think it has gone too far,' admitted Chatrier, himself the epitome of classic Parisian chic. 'To my eyes he looks ridiculous.' No more was said until the next morning's tabloids led with the story that henceforth Agassi might not be welcome at Roland Garros.

Goaded into a reply, Agassi called Chatrier 'a bozo' and said if he was not permitted to play in any clothes he chose then he would happily remain at home in Las Vegas where 'everybody dresses like this all the time'. Paris, like Melbourne and Wimbledon, would simply be erased from his schedule. 'It'll just be one less Grand Slam tournament to play in. You know, when it comes to Chatrier's benefit, tradition goes right out of the window,' he added in a carefully prepared statement. 'At Wimbledon there's only one sign on the Centre Court, a little Rolex watch sign. Here at Roland Garros there's not a single space without an advertisement of some sort. So you see, when Chatrier can reap the benefits, he doesn't care that much about tradition. Go ask the fans out there, they love something different. If I walked out in all white ninety-nine per cent of them would be disappointed. I want freedom to be what I want to be. Everyone in the world wants that except Philippe Chatrier.'

As the fortnight wore on, it began to look increasingly likely that the two fashion adversaries would come face to face on the trophy presentation catwalk, for the longer the tournament progressed, the more Agassi looked like the champion elect. Courier was despatched in the fourth round in the latest skirmish of their private war, Agassi losing the first set before obliterating his rival 6–7, 6–1, 6–4, 6–0. Chang, the defending champion, was similarly dismissed in the quarters, and Sweden's Jonas Svensson was beaten in a four-set semi-final victory which put Agassi into his first Grand Slam final.

His path to possible glory had not been without drama, however. Following his victory over Edberg at the Lipton International event in March, Agassi had competed in just one tournament out of eight and had flown into Charles de

Gaulle airport just twenty-four hours before his first-round match against Martin Wolstenholme, a 27-year-old Canadian ranked a lowly 122nd in the world and without any known form on European clay. On arrival at the airport, Agassi took one look at the courtesy car, a powerful new Peugeot 605, and insisted on taking the wheel and driving himself and companions into the centre of Paris. The chauffeur politely pointed out that this would not be possible owing to the difficulties of arranging adequate insurance cover at such short notice. According to the driver, an enraged Agassi promptly threw an almighty temper tantrum and insisted on calling the tournament office at Roland Garros where someone 'will sort this out in less than one minute flat'. He returned tight-lipped and slid, silently seething, into the back seat.

Short of sleep and short of temper, Agassi lost the first set to Wolstenholme on number one court at Roland Garros, earning as he did so a code violation warning from English umpire Sultan Ghangji for racquet abuse. During another heated outburst in the second set, Agassi called the umpire 'a little shit' and later demanded that he come down on the court to check a bounce mark in the clay. 'Get out of that damn chair right now!' he commanded. Agassi also deliberately hit Wolstenholme with one shot without apologising, a wanton act of vindictiveness which led the Canadian to say later: 'If I'd seen him in the locker room I'd have mentioned the incident. Hitting your opponent is legal, but it's a grey area of sportsmanship. He appears to be very hyper and very, very tense.'

With Ivan Lendl missing through injury, Mats Wilander in premature retirement and the top seeds Edberg and Becker victims of first-round defeats against Spaniard Sergi Bruguera and Croatia's Goran Ivanisevic respectively, the other finalist was Andres Gomez, Ecuador's greatest sporting hero, who had been a top-twenty player since 1982 but who had never been beyond the quarter-final of any Grand Slam championship since turning professonal in 1979. This was a classic Battle of Styles, because Gomez belongs to a bygone age. A huge, kindly bear of a man, the Ecuadorean is blessed with a touch as delicate as gossamer; he derives sheer delight from covering the whole court, which he regards as a sort of great canvas on which to paint his game, a lazy brushstroke here, a dab of colour there. To continue the artistic metaphor, if one was comparing their games one would say that Gomez works solely in pastel while Agassi works in spray-paint graffiti colours – fluorescent orange, pillar-box red, shocking pink, banana yellow.

To the delight of all in France over the age of twenty-one and especially, perhaps, to Monsieur Chatrier, Gomez, a part-time shrimp farmer, won 6–3, 2–6, 6–4, 6–4 to take the twenty-first, but by far the most important title of his noble career at the advanced age of thirty. As a visibly shocked Agassi hid his head in a towel by the umpire's chair, the immensely popular South American stood in a daze in the middle of the centre court. His tearfully jubilant wife Anna-Maria hugged their 24-month-old son Juan Andres junior and the Guayaquil ambassador to France leapt up and down in the VIP box like a three-year-old, waving a huge Ecuadorean flag. Actually, it was assumed to be the Ecuadorean flag, but no one really knew as it had never been seen at a French tennis tournament before.

After receiving the Musketeers Cup from 92-year-old Jean Borotra, champion in 1924 and 1931, Gomez smiled through the streaming tears and told the cheering crowd: 'I want to dedicate this victory to the people of my country, Ecuador. We are a very small nation, there are just 10 million of us, and it seems the only time we make headlines around the world is if there's an earthquake or something goes wrong with the government. This is a dream come true, and I mean those words from my heart. It's nice to do something that will make my people feel proud.' So proud, in fact, that when Gomez, Anna-Maria and little Juan Andres junior made a triumphal return to Guayaquil, their motorcade was brought to a standstill by over 100,000 cheering Ecuadoreans.

'I cried all the way into the capital,' added Gomez, who had been in such poor form before the tournament that he had seriously considered pulling out in order to commentate on Ecuadoran television. 'Then I heard Ivan [Lendl] had withdrawn, so I thought, "If Lendl's not going to Paris, I have as good a chance as anyone." So I told Anna-Maria, "Pack the bags. We will give it one last shot."'

For his part, having earlier hinted that he might recant and compete at Wimbledon for the first time since 1987, a bitterly disappointed Agassi disclosed he was too tired and 'still not physically strong enough. I need to get stronger.' Thus, as the world's top men and women tennis players descended upon Wimbledon for the 1990 championships, a confused young man duly went west again to nurse his bruised and battered ego, to rest and recuperate and to undergo an intensive spell of rigorous weight training under the relentless gaze of Gil Reyes. The only person who took the crushing defeat at Roland Garros even more painfully than Agassi was Bollettieri, who, on the day of the final, had told everyone in Paris who was prepared to listen: 'This is the day. This is the day I've been waiting thirty years for. Thirty years. You know, sometimes I wondered if this day would ever come.'

Agassi would spend five weeks in the Nevada Desert, during which time Edberg regained his Wimbledon crown by beating Becker in five sets, before returning to action in late July, winning in Washington but sustaining heavy defeats by Michael Chang, Australian Richard Fromberg and Sweden's Peter Lundgren in successive weeks. Of Fromberg Agassi had said: 'I can't get worked up to play guys like this every week.' The Australian was then ranked a highly respectable 24th in the world.

Australian broadcaster Craig Gabriel, a former ATP official, enjoys telling the story of a tetchy Agassi arriving in Cincinatti late one night and being met by a volunteer driver.

'I think we should slip out the back way,' Agassi advised the young woman seriously.

'And why is that?'

'Because I'll get mobbed if we walk through the airport.'

'Look Andre. This is Ohio, and it's eleven-thirty at night. Unless you've appeared on *Hee-Haw* recently [an American version of *Blue Peter*], no one here is going to give you a second look.'

The Fromberg defeat marked the end of a miserable week in Cincinatti, in which he was also fined $1,850 dollars for twice uttering the word 'fuck' on court. In eight tournaments he had been fined four times, for three 'fucks' and racquet throwing at Roland Garros, which suggested that however deep-felt his Christian beliefs might be, on court he remained the foul-mouthed tyke of old.

Agassi's mastery of Anglo-Saxon expletives should have led to his disqualification from the 1990 US Open at Flushing Meadow. Amid a heated exchange with Australian umpire Wayne McKewan over a disputed line call during his floodlit second-round encounter with Czechoslovak Petr Korda, Agassi received a warning for an audible obscenity after hurling his favourite expletive 'fuck' in McKewan's direction. Growing ever more vitriolic, Agassi continued his diatribe against the Australian sitting in the chair above his head. 'You sonofabitch!' he ended, and then spat, the spittle landing on McKewan's shoes and trousers. The umpire immediately called tournament supervisor Ken Farrar to the courtside and explained that he believed he had just been deliberately spat upon. Desperately trying to wriggle free from a moment of madness which could result in his immediate expulsion from the tournament, Agassi mounted a desperate plea for forgiveness: 'I spat on you? No. No, do you think I'd really do that? It was an accident. Really. Here, have my towel,' he begged, frantically trying to wipe the offending gob of spit from McKewan's toecap.

Farrar wrongly allowed Agassi to walk away without censure,

even though slow-motion replays provided by the USA Network television company clearly proved he had indeed spat, despite his continued protestations to the contrary. The supervisor later fined him $3,000 ($500 for saying 'fuck' and $2,500 dollars for spitting), some $2,000 below the disqualification limit. It was a decision Farrar was to rue when Agassi, who was booed when he walked out on court to play Argentina's Franco Davin in his next match, piously told a press conference: 'The whole thing wouldn't have happened if the umpire had been doing his job. The guy was looking for trouble. He was looking to start something with me. He had something against me from the start.'

Whatever problems he was having with officialdom, there was no doubting the potency of Agassi's tennis as he swept past Korda, Davin, Jay Berger and the new Russian number one, Andrei Cherkasov, to qualify for the semi-finals, where he would face title holder Boris Becker for the third succesive year. For once, Agassi gained inspiration from an early setback when, after saving four set points, the German won the 75-minute first set after a thrilling 22-point tie-break. The remainder of the match was an anti-climax, Agassi winning 6–7, 6–3, 6–2, 6–3 before celebrating his arrival in a second Grand Slam final by kneeling in prayer in the middle of the Stadium Court. Someone pointed out he was on almost the exact same spot of his disgusting tirade against McKewan ten days earlier.

As in Paris, Agassi, the favourite of both crowd and odds-makers, faced a younger opponent.

If you ever wonder what might have happened had Wimbledon welcomed the professional troupe in 1960 (when Pancho Gonzales ruled the paid circus with imperious authority) instead of 1968, you are likely to be given your answer one summer soon. Thirty years on, Pete Sampras is Gonzales in colour. The 21-year-old Greek-American still has much to learn in terms of subtlety and variety of shot, but the deceptively graceful 125 mph serve, the single panther-like bound to the net, the thumping forehand and the crackling-crisp volley are all vintage Gonzales. 'It is a little bit unnerving,' admits the Old One, who won the US championship at Forest Hills in 1948 and 1949. 'A couple of times when I've been following one of Pete's matches, I've adjusted the television controls and watched him in black and white. And I have to confess my heart always skips a beat or two.'

There is one glaring contrast between the two, however. Where Gonzales played each match as a man possessed in an era of impeccable decorum, Sampras displays not a sign of emotion at a time when many of his contemporaries view every umpire as a despised symbol of elderly authority. 'I suppose it's natural shyness, really,' he explains. 'My mom brought me up to have good manners on and off the tennis court. I guess I'd like to be remembered as a person who brought back the old-style game. A gentleman. The classic Mr Nice Guy.'

Though he is now firmly established as one of the best four or five players in the world, Sampras's early years as just-another-kid-with-a-two-fisted-backhand were spent as a support act to Agassi and Michael Chang, a position he might well have occupied to this day but for the percipience of his first coach, Dr Pete Fischer. Under the doctor's orders, Sampras abandoned his Bjorn Borg-style baseline game, and, inspired by videos of Gonzales, Rod Laver and Arthur Ashe, adopted the conventional backhand and attacking serve-volley style which surely mark him down as a future Wimbledon champion.

Sampras is a reluctant superstar, happy to remain unrecognised by the world at large. 'Sometimes, when I visit a fancy restaurant and I look at all the famous faces around me, I think to myself, "What on earth am I doing here?" I get terribly nervous if I feel people staring at me. I'm not really famous, I don't do anything really important in life, and I'm certainly not going to change the world, so I guess I feel uncomfortable when others treat me as though I'm special.' As someone who once, 'just once', hit a ball into the crowd in a silent show of temper, Sampras owes his self-effacing ways to his parents, Georgia and Soterios (Sam), who prefer to stay behind at home in Rancho Palos Verdes, California, rather than travel the world in his wake. Too nervous even to watch their son perform live on TV, they insist on hearing the results of important matches by way of long-distance telephone calls before turning on the video. Born in Sparta, Georgia has instilled the ancient virtues of honesty, modesty and generosity into her son.

After winning the stunning $2 million first prize in the inaugural Grand Slam Cup in Frankfurt three years ago, Sampras junior donated 25 per cent to a cerebral palsy charity. Typically, he made light of his gesture when it became public knowledge, saying: 'My dad's sister had cerebral palsy and when I was growing up he used to joke that if I ever won a lot of money it would be nice to donate a little bit of it to help fight the disease. It was no big deal.' Although he has since earned many millions, Sampras has never forgotten how to say 'thank you', and has even been known to drop a handwritten note to the behind-the-scenes staff at his favourite tournaments. 'As a tennis player we are mighty proud of him,' says Sam Sampras. 'As a son, our hearts are bursting.'

Sampras, seeded twelfth and bidding to become the youngest-ever winner of the US men's singles title, was in the middle of a scarcely believable streak; in the quarter-finals he overcame Ivan Lendl, a finalist at Flushing Meadow for the past eight years and champion on three occasions, 6–4, 7–6, 3–6, 4–6, 6–2, then subdued a rejuvenated John McEnroe, a four-times winner, 6–2, 6–4, 3–6, 6–3 with a fearsome display of power serving. He was not, however, expected to cope with an Agassi filled with desire to put the frustrations of Paris firmly behind him. Typically Bollettieri was in no doubt as to the outcome, repeating his performance at Roland Garros by telling all and sundry: 'Do you realise what day this is? Do you understand? Forget all about those other tournaments. Forget Wimbledon, forget the French. Andre's going to win the US Open right here in his own country.'

Agassi never even came close, being thrashed 6–4, 6–3, 6–2 with disdainful ease by Sampras. Sam and Georgia, sticking by their rule of never watching their son even on TV, happened upon on a TV set showing the awards ceremony in the department store in which they were browsing near their home in California. Agassi said he would like to take Sampras back to Las Vegas with him and turn him loose in Caesar's Palace: 'Everything he touched today turned to gold.' But he could not restrain himself from adding a sour note: 'But let's not get too carried away. Pete still has a lot to prove. The guy has a lot of tennis to play before we'll know just how good he really is.'

Sampras, who served 100 aces in his seven victories at Flushing Meadow, could not have cared less what Agassi thought. 'Whatever the future holds, I'll always have my US Open championship to look back on. But I have to admit Wimbledon is the one I really want. There's just so much history about the place it makes your skin tingle. I watch all the old tapes at home, particularly Rod Laver and that famous McEnroe–Borg final in 1980. All you can hear is the ball going back and forth, unlike at New York where all you can hear are the spectators. The silence sounds real nice. I guess it's because the people there have so much respect for the game. Wimbledon is somethimg I've dreamed of since I was a small boy, to join the legends.'

Despite the manner of his triumph, Sampras was not included in the team nominated by Tom Gorman for the Davis Cup semi-final with Austria in Vienna two weeks later. If his exclusion from a contest to be played on slow clay was no great surprise, the inclusion of Agassi after his spate of withdrawals and controversies was little short of astounding. At various times he had called Gorman a 'chameleon' and a 'glory hound', but under the personal orders of USTA chief David Markin,

Agassi was restored to the singles line-up along with Michael Chang. Aaron Krickstein, Brad Gilbert and Jay Berger, who had all performed with honour against Mexico and Czechoslovakia in the previous rounds, were cruelly overlooked. Eager to regain the trophy they had not held since 1982, the USTA welcomed the entire Agassi entourage without question while guaranteeing him a place in the squad for the final no matter how he performed in Vienna.

The two leading Austrians, Thomas Muster and Horst Skoff, have a well-publicised detestation of one another, but on a clay court specially laid in the national football stadium, and urged on by 17,000 Viennese voices, they formed a formidable alliance. The first day ended with honours even, Chang losing to the impressive Muster in four sets before Agassi levelled the score by beating Skoff for the loss of seven games. The Americans nudged ahead the following day when Rick Leach and Jim Pugh, the new Wimbledon doubles champions, overcame Muster and Alex Antonitsch. That night Agassi snubbed the official Davis Cup dinner, a long-established and popular tradition of the competition, as Mike Agassi so well remembers, in order to dine 'happy families style' with Phil, Bill, Gil and the rest of the jolly crew.

It was a calculated snub which angered Muster, who is among the most gentlemanly of individuals. He had hauled himself back to a world-ranked seventh after a horrific car accident in Miami the previous year when a drunk driver crashed into the front of the Austrian's car as he was loading the boot, pinning him underneath the wheels. Though the ligaments in his left knee were severed, Muster was playing again within six months, winning the 1990 Italian Open and reaching the semi-finals of the French Open. Nor was he intimidated by Agassi. 'I know exactly how to beat him. I really wanted him on the first day,' he said confidently before inflicting a thorough 6–2, 6–2, 7–6 whipping. Muster's twenty-fourth successive Davis Cup victory on clay levelled the match score at 2–2. Agassi, who had now lost three vital matches in the space of four months, to Gomez, Sampras and now Muster, reasoned: 'It was just nerves. I never promised anyone I would win.'

Fortunately for Markin and the USTA, Chang then recovered from two sets down to beat Skoff 3–6, 6–7, 6–4, 6–4, 6–3 in the deciding singles to give the Americans a narrow 3–2 overall victory and an engagement with Australia, who had thrashed Argentina 5–0 in the other semi-final, on an indoor clay court at St Petersburg, Florida, in December, when trouble continued to rumble all around Agassi like distant thunder. Having beaten the world's top two ranked players, Boris Becker and Stefan Edberg, on successive nights to win the first prize of $950,000 at the new end-of-season ATP Championships in Frankfurt, Agassi should have gone into the Davis Cup final in a positive frame of mind. Instead he struggled to overcome Richard Fromberg in five sets before disclosing he had been suffering from a 'horrible virus, had not eaten a bite for three days' and that his muscles hurt so much 'I couldn't roll over in bed'. He admitted he had not consulted a doctor and added needlessly: 'I guess even when I'm weak I'm less tired than him. I didn't win it with tennis, just guts.'

With standard Australian bluntness, Fromberg replied: 'Rubbish. I didn't see him sick during the match.' Ill or not, Agassi and his disciples sat eating in a restaurant that night until one in the morning. Even once the tie was decided, Chang thrashing Darren Cahill before the Americans won the doubles, Agassi continued to rub people the wrong way, quitting at one set apiece against Cahill in the first reverse singles claiming a pulled chest muscle. 'He didn't look injured to me hitting those groundstrokes,' derided the Australian. 'Andre is a great player but what comes out of his mouth is of little significance. I wouldn't want him on our team. Australians have a tradition, we go down fighting.'

The year duly ended as it had begun when Agassi, who had avoided the Australian Open that January, and sidestepped the

Grand Slam Cup staged in Munich at the end of December, a special tournament for the players who had performed best in the four Grand Slam championships. After entering, withdrawing and re-entering under threat of disciplinary action from the ITF, Agassi quit once more, pleading injury, and collected a $25,000 fine, a pittance to a man who had won $1,741,382 in prize money alone in 1990. Despite furnishing the ITF with three separate doctor's certificates, Agassi emerged with dishonour from the episode when a respected American journalist came forward to reveal how he had overheard Andre and Phil Agassi 'dream up' the injury scheme during dinner in a pancake house late one night.

In January 1991 the Australian Open was still deemed unworthy of Agassi's participation – the fifth straight year he had failed to show up in Melbourne – but his annual sabbatical failed to have the desired effect and the crushing defeats by Brad Gilbert, Germany's Christian Saceanu (world ranked 153), Courier and David Wheaton which followed suggested something was seriously wrong. In all, he suffered five first-round losses before he celebrated the return of the displaced Wendy Stewart into his life by winning the Orlando Classic in the Florida sunshine. In Paris in springtime Agassi, though he had slid alarmingly down the world rankings, rediscovered his very best form midway through the French Open, cuffing Argentine Alberto Mancini, Swiss Jakob Hlasek (for the loss of a mere five games) and Boris Becker to qualify for his third Grand Slam final and his second in a row on the clay courts of Roland Garros.

After what had been his fourth successive defeat against this denim-clad nuisance, Becker heaped praise upon his 7–5, 6–3, 3–6, 6–1 conqueror: 'Whether Andre wins or loses, he is always fair to me. As a player he is in a different league. He does not walk off court saying he is the greatest. He realises how close he came to losing today. He knows it's a matter of maybe one point. That is class. Andre is ready to win a Grand Slam, but he must keep his nerve.'

Awaiting Agassi in the most important match of his career – losing one major final could be construed as unlucky, losing two as carelessness, but losing three? – was his oldest and most bitter rival, Jim Courier, his one-time room-mate and sparring partner at Bollettieri's. The embers of their lingering enmity were fanned into life when Courier admitted he had quit Bollettieri's because he was tired of 'playing second fiddle'. 'Second fiddle?' sneered Agassi. 'Sounds like an insecurity problem to me.' To which Courier retorted: '*I'm* insecure?'

Whoever was the more insecure was irrelevant, Agassi was obviously the more nervous and it was Courier who won an error-strewn final 3–6, 6–4, 2–6, 6–1, 6–4 after his new coach Jose Higueras, during a rain break in the second set with Agassi one point away from a 4–1 lead, advised him to start standing ten feet behind the baseline to receive the Agassi serve. 'The pessimistic side of me now questions whether I'll ever win a Grand Slam championship,' confessed Agassi in a barely audible whisper after watching Courier clutch the magnificent Musketeers' Cup to his muscular chest. Slumped in a deep, black hole of despair, however, Agassi promised he would be at Wimbledon in two weeks' time and the tennis world held its breath. How would Nike find a way around the All England Club's stringent rules regarding coloured clothing?

On the eve of the championships, Agassi took time to reflect on his image: 'I'd like to be more popular but I don't know what else I can do. I believe in the Bible and read it every day, but that doesn't make me some kind of religious freak. Okay, I quit school early and had little formal education, but I'm not dumb. I like laughing and joking on court and having a bit of fun with the people out there, but that doesn't make me some kinda creepshow. I get a real positive response from the kids, the ones who come to see me play wearing all the Nike gear. But I guess their parents are suspicious since they're probably the ones paying out the money.'

As it happened, Agassi was a wow. When he sashayed out

on to the Centre Court for the first time to play Canadian Grant Connell he was bundled up under a floppy tracksuit which he slowly peeled away to reveal an outfit of the most dazzling white, albeit with familiar cycling shorts, also as pure as virgin snow, underneath. His tennis, too, was a revelation, even if he needed five sets to subdue Connell and another four to overcome Croatian Goran Prpic and advance to the third round. The whole nation warmed to this complex young man of twenty-one, and the admiration was mutual: 'Gee, this place really is something special,' enthused the white knight when he finally lost to fellow-American David Wheaton in an enthralling five-set quarter-final played before Princess Diana on the Centre Court. 'I can't wait for next year. It's definitely my all-time favourite place in the whole wide world.'

Though he won the Washington Classic from a weak field two weeks later, Agassi was finding it increasingly difficult to psyche himself up for the less important tour events. In the months following Wimbledon, he lost to Brad Gilbert, Petr Korda, French teenager Fabrice Santoro and Goran Ivanisevic before being drummed out of the 1991 US Open in straight sets in the first round by a mightily satisfied Aaron Krickstein. 'Wimbledon should have been my last hurrah for the year. I felt fried mentally after that. The French Open had also taken its toll on me. I almost felt like it wasn't worth ever getting to another final to feel that amount of pain if I lost. I had no motivation, no desire to dig right down and fight. I just wanted to get away.'

But after skipping the opening two rounds of the US defence of the Davis Cup, Agassi returned to duty and top form for the semi-final tie against Germany in Kansas City where he gave the Americans a tremendous start by whipping the new Wimbledon champion Michael Stich 6–3, 6–1, 6–4. With the match score level at 2–2, he then held his nerve to overwhelm Eric Jelen 6–2, 6–2, 6–3 to earn the US a 3–2 overall victory and a pre-Christmas jaunt to Lyon where Henri Leconte and Guy Forget of France were lying in wait.

The city of Lyon was never likely to open wide its arms, chirrup 'bonjour' and plant two Gallic smackers on the stubbled cheeks of Andre Agassi. Famous for the Michelin Guide quality of its restaurants (the region is known as the Kitchen of France), the number and diversity of its musuems (everything from marionettes to the history of the French Resistance) and its elegantly dressed citizenry, Lyon is recognised throughout France as the capital of sophistication. A typical Lyonaisse dinner party might consist of *émincé de filet de Charolais à la cailette de brebis et pomme de terre en robe du champ* (thinly sliced fillet steak served with a sausage of sheep's liver, offal, herbs, and a jacket potato), and a 1973 Pernand Vergelenes Côte de Beaune, all exquisitely served to the background accompaniment of Debussy. The talk will be of politics, the arts and mistresses in high places.

It is a world removed from that frequented by Agassi, a 21-year-old American who favours a single earring, colour uncoordinated ensembles resembling a double chocolate-chip ice-cream sundae, who lists his favourite author as: 'Don't have one, I never read books,' who patronises a Tex-Mex fast food chain called Taco Bell, who unwinds to Phil Collins and who rates Las Vegas 'the most beautiful city on earth'. Suddenly Agassi's sartorial inelegance was no longer the burning issue. The question mark hanging over his taste in clothes had been supplanted by the concern over his taste in food. Agassi had put on 20 pounds in the past year, whether by virtue of his quest in Gil Reyes' gymnasium to attain more upper body strength or his voracious appetite for junk food, no one was entirely certain.

Even on the long flight over to Lyon, Agassi, as prearranged with the airline, sat snuggled up to Wendy Stewart, devouring cokes and cheeseburgers. And although, no doubt in an effort to make up for his rudeness in Vienna, he attended the official Thanksgiving Dinner prepared by Paul Bocuse, the most celebrated chef in all France, Agassi spent much of the night complaining about the food and thereafter stuck rigidly to a diet of Big Macs and Mexican *fajitas*.

Though Agassi's individual performance was outstanding, the 1991 Davis Cup final ended in a crushing defeat for the United States. They were outsmarted, outfought and ultimately outplayed by a French team inspired by non-playing captain Yannick Noah, who had given up serious competition to launch a new career as a rock singer (his first single, 'Saga Africa', soared up the pop charts in France). Not since 1932 and the great days of the Four Musketeers, when France recorded the last of their six successive Davis Cup triumphs, had the country known such excitement and a joyously enthusiastic rabble of 8,000 packed into the Palais des Sports Gerland for the opening two singles.

The first match, Agassi v. Forget, was seen as the key to the entire final, and when the American managed to ignore the Gallic bedlam going on all about him and beat his opponent, ranked seventh in the world, by a score of 6–7, 6–2, 6–1, 6–2, there were smug smiles of satisfaction to be found wherever the Stars and Stripes fluttered around the arena. Next on to court were Pete Sampras, the 1990 US Open champion, and Henri Leconte, who, since humiliating Agassi four years earlier at Wimbledon, had undergone three back operations and plunged down the world rankings to 159th. A bon vivant of the old school, Leconte had been in enforced semi-retirement throughout the year and consequently looked distinctly puffy around the chest, thighs and waist. Indeed, as one observer noted, watching him pull on his tennis clothes in the locker room was like seeing Kim Basinger trying to squeeze into a pair of Twiggy's old jeans.

Sampras, still only twenty, may have been a veteran of Flushing Meadow, but he had never encountered anything like the atmosphere in Lyon that night. Amid repeated choruses of *La Marseillaise*, Leconte rolled back the years with a sumptuous display, winning 6–4, 7–5, 6–4 in what he was to call 'the most complete match of my life'. 'Henri was dead,' said Noah. 'To live again he needed a dream. I have given him a dream.' The following afternoon Leconte continued his magnificent comeback when he joined with Forget to defeat Ken Flach and Robert Seguso in four sets, only their second reversal in twelve Davis Cup doubles. Miraculously, France were 2–1 in front with the two reverse singles to come on the final day.

To the crowd's roars of '*Allez*! *Allez*! *Allez*!' Forget whipped the nerve-wracked Sampras in four sets, leaving Noah all but speechless for the first time in his life. 'I don't think the Americans realised how much the Davis Cup means to the French team and the French people. In America they have ten different things that are more important than the Davis Cup.'

Though he had won the United States' sole point in the 3–1 defeat, Agassi's year had again ended in anti-climax. Another million or so in prize money, plus many more millions in endorsement fees, he had almost slipped out of the world's top ten for the first time since early 1988, and was still without a Grand Slam title to his name, while Sampras, Courier and Chang boasted one apiece. 'I think that bugs him a little,' noted Sampras with classic understatement.

Nor did the first six months of 1992 suggest anything other than a gradual slide into wealthy obscurity. The Australian Open came and went without him for the sixth year in a row, and there swiftly followed a rush of defeats against such support acts as Switzerland's Jakob Hlasek (Milan, first round), Russian Alexander Volkov (Brussels, second round), Swiss Marc Rosset (Scottsdale, second round), American Bryan Shelton (Key Biscayne, second round), Dutchman Jacco Eltingh (Barcelona, second round) and Argentine Franco Davin (Tampa, quarter-finals), the last three ranked 71st, 110th and 111th in the world respectively. By the time of the French Open in June, Agassi's own world ranking, which had stood at number 3 in January 1989, had slumped to 17 by the spring of 1992 and was dropping fast; he had also experimented with different strings in his racquet, various tensions, tinkered with his serve and footwork, hired and fired an assistant coach to teach him how to volley, then embarked upon and abandoned a specially formulated low-fat diet.

'I go through stages these days where it seems no one can beat me, then it seems anyone can beat me,' Agassi admitted in a rare moment of introspection. 'I appear to have been playing horribly for an eternity. I sometimes wonder if I'm capable of hitting the ball, or if I'll ever win a tournament or even a single match again.' The root of all his problems, so Agassi believed, had been his five-set defeat by Courier at Roland Garros twelve months before. 'It felt so unfair. Paris didn't just leave me with doubts, it almost destroyed my confidence.'

Strangely, whilst his fortunes had dipped, Agassi remained the focus of all attention at Roland Garros last summer. Whereas John McEnroe had been a latter-day Bob Dylan in sneakers, an irreverent spokesman for the youth of his day, a puzzlement to the middle-aged middle class, Agassi was a punk. The older generation reviled him because of his loud clothes, earrings, peroxide tresses and outrageous behaviour, and their teenage offspring adored him for exactly the same reasons. But all the while Agassi was becoming an icon of the 1990s, and a multimillionaire, Jim Courier was nursing his resentment. Like a gathering storm he plodded his way up the world rankings: 348th . . . 207th . . . 111th . . . 80th . . . 24th . . . 12th . . . to his then current place at the very top of the heap.

Courier, winner of the 1992 Australian Open at Flinders Park that January, cruised into the semi-finals of the French Open with a series of impressively muscular displays, as Agassi, recapturing some of the old magic, won five matches for the loss of just one set to earn another crack at his former room-mate. In front of his deathly pale entourage – Bollettieri in particular looked like a man attending his own funeral – Agassi was utterly outclassed 3–6, 2–6, 2–6. Courier went on to retain the French crown, his third Grand Slam title, while an influential American magazine posed the vexed question 'Agassi – A Born Loser?', in which the author listed his reasons why the Las

Vegan, still only twenty-one, was doomed never to win a major championship.

'It didn't make me angry, merely more determined. Let's face it, I'd already achieved more than most players by reaching the finals of the French and two U.S. Opens. If I'd died then and never played another match my record would have stood the test of time. But when I next saw the writer I said: "A born loser? Come back and see me in ten years' time if I still haven't won a French or a US or, best of all, a Wimbledon championship."'

6

The White Knight

The ludicrously brief interval between the French Open and Wimbledon is always a time of frenetic activity as the players, the great and the humble alike, endeavour to adjust mind and body to the peculiar demands of playing tennis on grass. There are but fourteen days to prepare for the fortnight of crash-bang-wallop to come on the hallowed and high-speed lawns of the All England Club after the months of patient toil on the slow clay courts of Barcelona, Nice, Monte Carlo, Madrid, Hamburg, Dusseldorf, Rome and Paris, where exhausting baseline rallies of fifty-plus strokes are not uncommon.

This abrupt switch from the terracotta-coloured clay of Paris, which the French call *terre battue* (crushed earth) to grass is roughly the equivalent of driving from the sands of the Sahara straight out on to a greasy skid-pan. Few people ever negotiate the crossing without an audible screech of tyres.

In fact, since the Second World War, just five men have won the French Open and the Wimbledon crown in the same summer – Americans Budge Patty (1950) and Tony Trabert (1955), Australia's Lew Hoad (1956) and Rod Laver (1962 and 1969), and the remarkable Bjorn Borg of Sweden (1978–1980).

But that select quintet all belonged to an earlier innocent age. As the modern game became increasingly dominated by power, so the feeling grew that as far as future Wimbledons were concerned, only hulking giants standing 6 feet 3 inches and over and armed with wide-bodied racquets and turbo-charged serves need apply.

In the summer of 1992 therefore, three-times champion Boris Becker and twice-winner Stefan Edberg appeared to pose the main threat to title holder Michael Stich, with Pete Sampras, Goran Ivanisevic and the fast-emerging South African Wayne Ferreira and Richard Krajicek of the Netherlands forming a second wave of robust challengers. Andre Agassi, according to most expert opinion, lacked the required physique, the 125 mph cannonball first serve and the instinctive volley needed to make a major impact on what would be only his third appearance on Wimbledon grass. This school of thought chose to overlook the fact that Borg had been perceived as being similarly deficient but had managed to remain on the baseline while winning five successive men's singles titles between 1976 and 1980 on the strength of his astonishingly accurate and fearsomely struck groundstrokes.

Like Borg, Agassi came to Wimbledon possessed of an adoring fan club of teenyboppers, a venomous double-fisted backhand, a forehand which positively crackled with menace, plus a much improved volley as a result of the hours of practice he had put in throughout the season under the expert tutelage of John McEnroe. The one-time antagonists were by now firm friends, even forming a 'dream team' in Paris, where they had reached the quarter-finals of the French Open men's doubles amid frenzied crowd scenes.

'You've no idea how much I learned from just watching the man up close,' says Agassi with genuine awe in his voice. 'I remember a point in our very first match at Roland Garros when one of our opponents, Todd Nelson I think, attempted a trick shot – you know the type, a real cute cross-court volley which ran along the top of the net. I didn't even notice John move, but by the time the ball landed he was standing there waiting to put it away for a clean winner. As he passed my shoulder he muttered out the side of his mouth, "I've been around way too long to fall for that one." When it comes to tennis, John McEnroe has probably forgotten more than the rest of us put together will ever know.'

Rebuilt volley or not, if Agassi was indeed serious in his oft-stated intent of launching a determined assault on Wimbledon in 1992, it was generally assumed he would head straight to London from Paris for the prestigious Stella Artois tournament, which is played on the slick turf of Queen's Club. The list of past champions there spans the Hall of Fame generations: Tilden and Crawford, Budge and von Cramm, Hoad and Rosewall, Laver and Emerson, Newcombe and Smith, Connors and McEnroe, Edberg and Becker.

However, although the organisers reserved a place in the draw until the very last moment, Agassi sidestepped Queen's Club, obviously feeling it was still too early to reveal his hand to his main rivals. Nor did he accept the various other invitations on offer to snatch some much-needed grass court practice in the less intimidating surroundings of the other warm-up events being staged at Beckenham, Manchester and Hoylake, or at Rosmalen in the Netherlands.

No, after his crushing defeat against Jim Courier at Roland Garros, Andre Agassi chose to prime himself for the lush green grass of Wimbledon by ignoring all such opportunities and flying home to Las Vegas, that neon oasis of peace and tranquillity in the middle of the Nevada Desert, via Florida. When he did find time to hit a tennis ball on the final days leading up to Wimbledon, he did so on an air-conditioned indoor court, but for much of the fortnight he blithely concentrated on honing his eight-handicap golf swing (he plays left-handed, incidentally) on the beautifully manicured fairways of the Spanish Trail Country Club.

This apparent indifference to the challenge ahead was misleading, because although the first six months of 1992 had been a particularly miserable spell in terms of results, Agassi was approaching Wimbledon with a sense of real optimism rather than an air of foreboding. After all, had he not led fellow-American and former fellow-Bollettieri student David Wheaton by two sets to one in the quarter-finals twelve months earlier before finally submitting when hampered by a thigh injury?

'People forget that with a bit of luck in 1991 I could have been playing for the Wimbledon championship against Michael Stich,' he explained on the eve of the 106th championships. 'This year I'll be stepping out on the Centre Court with a heap more confidence. No longer do I feel I'll be running the risk of being run over by anyone. I just know I'm going to feel a lot more comfortable with the whole scene – the crowds, the pressure, the sense of history. No way will I feel intimidated. This time I'll feel enthused. At any run-of-the-mill tournament I kinda feel like the underdog, even when I'm playing well. I guess I surprise myself when I win. But when any one of the Grand Slams rolls around, I immediately become arrogant, confident, like I'm unbeatable or something.'

And in an uncannily accurate prediction of the events to come, Agassi went on: 'Of course Wimbledon is by far the most difficult of the four Grand Slam championships for me to win because it's played on grass. Obviously the surface does favour the recognised serve-volleyers, but it's not too hard to hold serve on grass, even for me. The key is how often I can break my opponent. I feel I return well enough to keep up the pressure on even the biggest servers – Becker, Ivanisevic, Sampras, Stich. By no means would I be favoured to beat Becker on the Centre Court, say, but he wouldn't walk out there thinking he has the match won for sure either.'

Even once he was settled in London, Agassi continued to scorn the chance of practice on the grass courts reserved for the Wimbledon players in the adjacent Aorangi Park complex, though he was spotted undergoing a rigorous work out with McEnroe hidden away from public gaze on an outside court at Queen's Club. For most of the time, however, he belted groundstrokes on one of the All England Club's indoor courts. 'The bounce on an artificial court is always 100 per cent true, which is more than you can say for grass. There's no way I can groove my game on grass. In fact, I find the more time I spend on the stuff the worse I play.'

But despite this bravado, some would say heresy, by the time the draw for the men's singles was announced, it was patently clear to his nearest and dearest that Agassi was growing more nervous by the hour. Meals were left uneaten, conversations left unfinished, movies left unwatched. The pressure to win a major championship, to prove Andre Agassi was as good a tennis player as his publicity machine was over-fond of claiming, was gradually mounting.

Nor did fortune smile benignly upon the number twelve seed, according him the dubious reward of an opening match against the immensely talented but infuriatingly inconsistent Andrei Chesnokov, appearing for the first time under the banner of the Commonwealth of Independent States. Though the Russian had never progressed beyond the first round in three previous visits to the All England Club, he had been ranked as high as ninth in the world just fourteen months earlier and is generally considered to be a man best avoided whatever the tournament, whatever the surface.

Ever loyal, Phil Agassi attempted to reassure his younger brother by pointing to the fact that the Muscovite 'might be a danger on clay or carpet, but had never done anything at all on grass'. 'No. And nor have I,' came the brutally honest rejoinder.

With Chesnokov, who has been famously described as a Marxist of the Groucho Tendency, one never knows. When the mood is upon him he can embarrass the very best in the world with his penchant for hitting outrageous winners from every corner of the court; another day, another place, he is a clown in tennis whites, incapable of making even the most simple return without falling on his face. On court or off, however, he is never less than entertaining company, though it is often difficult to tell when he is joking and when he is being serious.

For example, he blamed an unexpected defeat in Monte Carlo on the new shoes he had been supplied with by the notoriously miserly Soviet Tennis Federation, which used to relieve Chesnokov of 90 per cent of his earnings. 'I never wear again. But, no, I not throw away, I find good use for them. What? I make soup. Yes. You ever taste Russian soup? I tell you, these shoes will make better soup than Russian cabbage.'

To the continuing dismay and puzzlement of his clean-living contemporaries, the Russian mocks the Spartan regime of the athlete, that monastic life comprised entirely of early-morning runs, vitamin-controlled diets and monotonous practice drills. Like most of his fellow-countrymen, Chesnokov enjoys his beer and the 'occasional vodka'. He also confesses to a liking for black caviare, a thrash heavy metal rock group called Death Wish Destruction and 'pretty girls from east or west. I have no preference. I like to meet all kinds.'

To the despair of his long-suffering coach ('and my very best friend') Tatiana Naoumko, Chesnokov, who takes great delight in roaring around the streets of Rome bareheaded on his motorbike every year during the Italian Open, much prefers discos, chess, philately, browsing in bookshops or just watching the world go lazily by from a pavement cafe to time spent on a tennis court practising his double-fisted backhand.

'Ah, but in Rome one year I prove something,' explained this master of the illogical. 'First night I have dinner with my coach, and go to bed early. I read. I sleep. Next day I play terrible. That night I run away from Tatiana. I go dancing, I drink beer, I meet nice Italian girls. I go to bed late, I do not practise. Next day I play great. You see? So now you tell me, where is best disco in Wimbledon?'

There were times during their first-round encounter on Wimbledon's number one court (played over two days due to a rain delay) when Chesnokov looked as though he must have danced the previous night away, and Agassi was mightily relieved to squeeze into the second round after a hard-fought 5–7, 6–1, 7–5, 7–5 victory. 'I was very, very nervous,' he admitted. 'But it's good to come through such a tough first-round match and not feel fatigued. Chessie is just about the very last person you want to have to play in the first round of Wimbledon. He can simply blow you away, whoosh, just like that. I guess playing doubles with John [McEnroe] at the French Open really helped because I was very confident when I came up to the net even on crucial points. I know what I'm saying is only based on this one match, but I do feel the volley is gradually becoming second nature to me.'

However, Agassi's new-found self-assurance on grass was merely a side issue to the burning question of the day, had tennis's golden boy suddenly taken to wearing a white baseball cap on court to camouflage the fact that he was rapidly going bald? 'Oh really? Is that what they're saying? It's just my lucky hat, that's all. I wore it in Paris and it treated me well enough, so I'm hoping it will carry me through Wimbledon. Also, I'm growing my hair at the sides and it's difficult to keep it all under control with a simple headband.'

To emphasise the point, the flowing Agassi tresses were left uncovered when he walked out on court to face Argentine-born Belgian Eduardo Masso in his next match. Like Chesnokov, Masso, who is married to a glamorous Brussels fashion model, had arrived at the 1992 Wimbledon championships without a single victory on grass on his CV, an omission he quickly put to rights when he somewhat surprisingly overcame Swedish qualifier Niclas Kroon 6–7, 6–4, 6–2, 2–6, 6–4 in a first-round encounter played out before a handful of spectators enjoying a quiet Tupperware lunch on an outside court.

Though he is perhaps best known on the circuit for an idiosyncratic habit of bouncing the ball on the edge of his racquet frame several times before throwing it up to serve, Masso is a wily opponent and his cunning mixture of lobs, drop-shots and assorted spins threw Agassi into total confusion in the first set, which the Belgian duly won 6–4. 'He surprised me in that first set. You know, I think when you come to Wimbledon you are so pumped up that you have an incredible amount of energy when you finally go out to play. Then when you have to come right back out the very next day, maybe against someone less well known like Masso, it always takes just that little while longer to get your act together.'

Immediately donning his 'lucky' white cap at the start of the second set, Agassi required scarcely more than another hour to solve Masso's mysteries, racing through the remainder of the match for the loss of just seven games before the subject again returned to the Fleet Street-inspired rumour that his hair was fast going the way of brother Phil's toupee, 'the Persian Rug'.

'You know these stories only ever arise in Britain. Yesterday everyone was saying, "Why are you wearing the cap? We want to see your hair." It was kinda like when I took to wearing sunglasses on court. Every now and then, I think people want to see a change, so that's why I wore the headband today. When I started losing, I panicked, so I put the hat back on.'

The rumours, like Agassi's patience, were never-ending, however. From the locker room came tales that certain mischievous rivals had pasted up adverts for hair restorer on his locker, while American TV chat show host Dennis Miller started an 'Andre watch' by inviting members of his audience to send in pictures of the infamous 'bald patch'.

More seriously, the next opponent to heave into Agassi's view was Derrick Rostagno, who was widely feared as one of the most dangerous 'floaters' in the Wimbledon draw. In 1990, the

26-year-old Californian had outplayed John McEnroe 7–5, 6–4, 6–4 in the first round, and twelve months later, when he would end the year ranked thirteenth in the world, he thrashed Pete Sampras and Jimmy Connors for the loss of just one set to reach the last sixteen, thereby becoming only the third player after Bjorn Borg and big-serving South African Kevin Curren to chalk up career victories over both Connors and McEnroe at Wimbledon.

Born in Hollywood, Rostagno led something of a hippy existence in his early years on the professional tour when he travelled, ate, and slept in a beat-up Volkswagen caravanette, preferring to strum 1960s 'flower power' songs on his guitar by the warm glow of a campfire to the perceived luxury of a five-star hotel room. Once, after losing in the early rounds of a tournament at Brindisi, he worked as a garage repairman for the rest of the week to 'learn Italian and have a bit of fun', and was often known to hitchhike from one venue to the next.

Much of his carefree attitude can be traced back to a tragic accident in 1986 when a Mexicana Airlines flight on which he was booked to fly from Mexico City to Los Angeles exploded shortly after take-off, killing 150 passengers and crew. Rostagno had actually travelled on the plane from Guadalajara and was about to reboard the doomed aircraft for the last leg of his journey home when he learned of a tournament being staged in the Mexican capital. It was only while waiting in the departure lounge that he decided to postpone his return and remain behind.

'When that sort of thing happens, I guess you come to see the occasional setback on the tennis court for what it really is. It didn't change my life or anything, but it was as though I'd been handed a very special gift. It's still nice to walk off a tennis court as the winner, but a disaster like that sure puts defeat into perspective.'

That philosophical outlook stood Rostagno in good stead against Boris Becker in the second round of the 1989 US Open, when he held two match points in the fourth set before going down 6–1, 7–6, 3–6, 6–7, 3–6 in four hours and twenty-seven minutes. He lost the second point on the most freakish of net-cords, when the German's desperate return clipped the very top of the tape and flew high over the Californian's head as he waited for the kill.

Though Rostagno never looked capable of threatening Agassi's ambitions, his classic – if deceptively gentle – serve-volley style offered the Las Vegan the perfect opportunity to test his baseline counter-attack tactics against a highly qualified net-rusher. 'People kept telling me what an easy ride I was having,' laughs Agassi, who secured his place in the fourth round with an impressive 6–3, 7–6, 7–5 victory. 'But I sure didn't see it that way at the time. A few points either way against Chesnokov and I could have gone out in the first round, and Rostagno is one smooth operator at Wimbledon. That was an important win for me because that's when it really hit me that I could play my own game and compete with the very best on grass. That I didn't have to go up to the net unless I really wanted to, that I had the shots to threaten anyone's serve, that my own serve was reasonably secure.'

While Agassi had been plotting a relatively trouble-free passage to the fourth round, his projected opponent in the last sixteen, sixth-seeded Czechoslovak Petr Korda, had unexpectedly run aground against Prague-born Swiss Jakob Hlasek. Runner-up to Courier in the French Open, Korda had won the first two sets of a thrilling second-round contest out on Court 13 before his opponent staged a remarkable recovery to win 4–6, 3–6, 6–3, 7–6, 16–14. Hlasek was something of a grass court specialist and had broken into the world's top ten in 1988. He loomed ominously on Agassi's horizon until like Korda he too went out in the most unexpected manner to Germany's Christian Saceanu.

Born in Klausenburg, Romania, Saceanu had moved to Germany with his family when he was fifteen to further his tennis career and immediately attracted the attention of Gunther

Bosch, the astute coach who had fashioned a world champion out of the youthful Boris Becker. 'Considering the poor quality of the facilities in Romania, and his lack of experience in international competition, Saceanu really was a tremendous prospect as a teenager,' recalls Bosch. 'He wasn't another Becker – then who was? – but he definitely had the potential to be a top-twenty player.'

However, Bosch was to discover that although you can take the boy out of Romania, you can never quite take Romania out of the boy; Saceanu's idol, it transpired, was Ilie Nastase. Like his hero, the talent was glorious, but the temperament fragile.

Now nine years on, the pair had long since dissolved their partnership, Bosch to seek a new champion from the hundreds of German youngsters attracted into tennis by the deeds of Becker and Steffi Graf, Saceanu to become an anonymous if noisome member of the tour's chorus line. At the end of 1992 he ranked sixtieth in the world, though he had beaten Agassi at the Donnay Indoor Championship in Brussels and reached the third round at Wimbledon. Then, following a miserable run of eleven first-round defeats in thirteen events, he dropped off the top 200 on the computer and was required to pre-qualify for the 1992 championships.

Overnight, Saceanu, who had won two grass court titles during his career, the same meagre total, incidentally, as Pat Cash, Ivan Lendl and Michael Stich, mysteriously rediscovered his old touch, racing through the Wimbledon qualifying tournament at Roehampton before advancing to the fourth round proper with a series of startling performances. After beating Gabriel Markus in the first round, one of the rising stars of Argentine tennis, Saceanu had been involved in a minor classic against Frenchman Cedric Pioline from which he eventually emerged triumphant by a fluctuating score line of 4–6, 6–4, 0–6, 7–5, 7–5.

Though often sparkling, the tennis on court nine that balmy June afternoon in no way matched the drama of the players. Pioline plays tennis the way most Italians drive, that is to say he screamed, he gesticulated, threw tantrums, beseeched the gods and cast muttered imprecations in the direction of the umpire. That said, in contrast to Saceanu, he was serenity personified.

'What you expect?' demanded a genuinely puzzled Saceanu, who carved his own little niche in Wimbledon folklore by being asked to turn down the volume by English umpire Jeremy Shales, who was actually officiating at a match involving Frenchman Thierry Champion and Mexico's Leonardo Lavalle on the adjoining court. 'I'm from Romania, just like Nastase. I serve a double fault on match point and the umpire says, "Sssh". How can you "Sssh", how can you keep your emotions under control at such a moment?' asked the Romanian, who had marked that particular incident by attempting to smash the umpire's chair into firewood with his racquet.

'It's not just me, it's all Romanians act this way. We're like the Italians, you know, only a bit more emotional maybe. Is good for the crowds, yes? That's why everyone love Nastase, because he always opens up his heart and soul on the tennis court.'

Thus, after outlasting Hlasek in his second successive five-setter, it was the impassioned Saceanu who obstructed Agassi's route to the quarter-finals as the championships entered their second week. But, as against Rostagno in the previous round, the American rose to the peak of his powers, winning a more than useful work out 7–6, 6–1, 7–6. While his serve was delivered with zip, and his groundstrokes with power and precision, it was Agassi's ability to play what the professionals term the 'big points' which most impressed seasoned observers. The two tie-breaks, potential minefields both, were secured for the aggregate loss of just one point.

'I hope he does win Wimbledon this year,' said Saceanu of his conqueror, 'because if you must lose, it's always better to lose to the eventual champion. I don't think I have ever served or volleyed better, but I tell you, some of his returns were out of this world. I only saw Borg on television, but I cannot believe he was more powerful or more accurate than Andre from the baseline.'

Now Agassi's greatest Wimbledon challenge lay ahead, a quarter-final engagement with Boris Becker, three times champion and a finalist for six of the past seven years on the Centre Court, a patch of greensward the German habitually referred to as 'my back garden'.

It was then seven years since Becker had first descended upon the All England Club like a strawberry-blond tornado, becoming the first German, the first unseeded player and the youngest competitor ever to win the men's singles when he beat Kevin Curren in the 1985 final. As well as spawning a massive trade in B-shaped sugar-coated doughnuts in his homeland, he inspired a whole new newspaper vocabulary as fitting words and phrases were invented to accommodate him: 'Borissimo', 'Boom Boom' and, of course, the favoured soubriquet of the Fleet Street tabloids, 'Bonking' Boris. Tennis, originally the sport of the landed gentry, had been transformed into pure soap opera.

But fame and fortune had failed to bring lasting contentment, as Becker revealed with the surprising disclosure: 'Shall I tell you my secret? If I were granted a belated wish, I would wish I had mis-hit that match point against Curren in the Wimbledon final. Of course, the seventh day of the seventh month of 1985 was a fantastic day for me. Since then seven is always my lucky number, but this damned luck is also my damned misfortune because the life that overwhelmed me afterwards simply could not be handled by a seventeen-year-old. I was continually forced to play a role I did not want to play. I was trapped in a substitute life in which I was completely identified with tennis and which turned me into a person I'm not.'

Contrary to the visual evidence and the vibration in the stands at Wimbledon when a serve is being delivered, Becker's most vital strength lies not in his redoubtable physique, but in his brain. 'He's controversial, different, human, versatile, but most of all intelligent,' says Ion Tiriac, his brooding Romanian manager, who cultivates a Transylvanian-style drooping moustache and a Machiavellian image. 'His mother is a very strong-minded person and he gets his dedication from her. His Latin side, his romantic side, he inherits from his father.'

Unlike many of his contemporaries, who see tennis, and, by logical extension, money as their sole reason for existence, Becker's millions have always rested uneasily on his shoulders. He is a young man who is genuinely distressed by illness, famine and poverty. At one time he refused to represent Germany in the Davis Cup because he was disgusted by the excesses of the corporate caviare brigade who were fast taking over the courtside seating. He has publicly ridiculed the new wave of neo-Nazis, renounced national service and moved to Monte Carlo for cosmopolitan as well as tax purposes, saying he passionately believes he is a citizen of the world rather than a German.

'I am really surprised I am so popular in Germany because I have big problems with the German mentality. I am more in favour of the easy-going, uncomplicated way of artists. I think I could understand the stars, Marlene Dietrich, for example, who fled abroad to get away from the German mentality.'

Generous in victory, Becker has long been renowned in the locker room for his graciousness in defeat. After the little-known Australian Peter Doohan had ended his bid for a third successive Wimbledon crown in 1987 with a stunning upset victory on number one court, the nineteen-year-old Becker refused to describe the result as a disaster: 'It's not a tragedy,' he said softly. 'No one died out there. It isn't war, you know.'

Now asked if he had any advice to offer the likes of Agassi, Ivanisevic, Sampras and Ferreira, all of whom were being touted as future Wimbledon champions, Becker issued this sombre warning: 'I woke up next morning and I was famous; everybody in the world knew me, my face was in every newspaper and magazine. Can you imagine what it is like to go to bed one person and wake up a new human being?

'I have now become a peacock and, as a peacock, am never given one minute's peace, even in restaurants. The tourists stare at me, the customers at the next table whisper and it's not only the Japanese who take photographs of me all the time. My problem, which drives me mad at times, is that I am working practically twenty-four hours a day, and that has been true for seven or eight long years. I can never shake off this Becker, not even after the work is done. Round the clock, I am this chap with the famous blue eyes, always and always this guy who is treated like a mascot by the people.'

Nor can the earnest Becker be accused of exaggerating his own importance, for, as a recent survey conducted by a German newspaper discovered, he is better known than their own head of state. He had a recognition rate of 97 per cent, higher than Chancellor Kohl, golfer Bernhard Langer, national soccer captain Lothar Matthaeus, higher even than Fraulein Forehand, Steffi Graf.

But despite his humility, Becker is a dichotomous creature, frequently guilty of trying to unsettle opponents, especially at his beloved Wimbledon, by gamesmanship, his very physical presence, the force of his personality or by sheer bully-boy tactics. 'Yes. There is nothing I wouldn't do on court in order to win,' he agrees.

This drive for superiority was hatched in early childhood when he was forced to play with Steffi Graff because she was the best of the girls and he was the worst of the boys. Tiriac remembers him as 'lumpy and slow'. Becker remembers the mockery: 'The older players often made fun of me. At the time I swore that one day I would sweep all these twits away. This feeling of bitter resentment stayed with me, and now my opponents are on the receiving end of it, even though they themselves have done me no harm. There is no cure for this fever.'

If there is a hunger more acute than the desire for vengeance gnawing away at Becker, it can only be his appetite for theatricality, one reason perhaps why he describes his relationship with tennis fans as erotic. 'In my best games my bond with the public is certainly erotic. A five-hour match in front of 20,000 New Yorkers in the evening atmosphere of Flushing Meadow is like an act of love for me. They want your body and they want your soul. And as in love, the pleasure in a big fight begins with the foreplay, with the first eye contact, and so on until finally we melt into one another, the public into me and I into the public.'

But the Becker awaiting Agassi on the Centre Court on the afternoon of Wednesday 1 July was riddled with self-doubt. Since winning his first Australian Open title in January 1991, the German had suffered a dismal run of 'failures' in the four great Grand Slam championships: 1991 French Open, lost to Agassi, semi-finals; 1991 Wimbledon, lost to Stich, final; 1991 US Open, lost to Haarhuis, third round; 1992 Australian Open, lost McEnroe, third round; and 1992 French Open, withdrew injured.

Nor had he looked the fearsome gladiator of old in the early rounds at Wimbledon, needing a total of fourteen gruelling sets to overcome Czechoslovak teenager Martin Damm, American Bryan Shelton and Wayne Ferreira, the number fourteen seed from Johannesburg.

On the night before their eagerly awaited Wimbledon quarter-final contest – billed the 'heavyweight championship of Wimbledon' by the delighted pack of ticket touts plying their trade outside the Fred Perry gates – Agassi had dinner at the Hard Rock Cafe in Park Lane with McEnroe and plotted the German's downfall. 'John really helped me in terms of strategy throughout the championship. I had this habit of hitting what you might call "neutral" shots like I'd do on clay. He made me realise grass isn't like that. At Wimbledon, every shot you hit counts, and if you don't put everything into every stroke of every rally, there's a good chance you're going to lose every point.'

By any standards, Agassi and Becker, again without a coach

at the time following a difference of opinion with former Czechoslovak Davis Cup stalwart Tomas Smid, combined to produce one of the truly outstanding contests of the year. The German was at times simply irresistible. With his Wagnerian serve he muscled his way through the first set. Agassi then let loose a stream of unanswerable forehand and backhand winners, the like of which had not been seen on the Centre Court since the days of Borg some fifteen years before.

As darkness and rain fell in unison, the two players scampered off, to a standing ovation from a spellbound audience. The lights of the scoreboard, standing out in the gloom, showed Agassi ahead 4–6, 6–2, 6–2.

Incredibly, both the former champion and the champion-to-be moved on to another level of play when it was resumed on the Thursday afternoon. Despite his reputation as a notoriously slow starter, it was an inspired Becker who seized the initiative with a vintage display of serve-volleying which brought him the fourth set 6–4. The tension on Centre Court reached almost unbearable heights.

To his credit, it has to be said that Becker played the fifth set with unvarying intensity. However, Agassi, already performing unbelievably well, began playing the very best tennis of his life. The German's awesome serves were returned with something approaching nonchalance, his volleys contemptuously sent back as outright winners or wonderfully disguised lobs. As brilliantly as he played, the 1985, 1986 and 1989 champion found himself trailing 5–1 before Agassi, showing the first understandable signs of nerves, double faulted to drop his serve for the first time in the fifth set.

At 5–3 there was to be no such hiccup and the two great rivals joined together in an embrace of mutual respect as a crescendo of noise reverberated around the historic stadium.

'No matter how many important matches I win, that will undoubtedly remain one of the greatest achievements of my career,' says Agassi looking back on that memorable afternoon.

'You can never feel confident about playing Becker, especially at Wimbledon where he seems to grow six inches when you look at him across the net. He'd been in the last five finals and six out of the last seven, so although I'm not certain it felt more special than the other times I'd beaten him, it was certainly more of an accomplishment.'

Even after an interval of twelve months, Becker finds it difficult to explain why Agassi, who had then beaten him on six successive occasions, appears to gain inspiration from their meetings. 'You have to ask him, I think. He is playing the whole year not great and then whenever he sees my face on the tennis court, he starts playing two classes better than against anybody else. It was not a matter of me playing bad against Agassi at Wimbledon last year. It was one of the best, if not the best, games of the tournament for me, you know. I was all the time there mentally. I was serving good, I was playing good. I did not hit a bad shot. He hit some shots which were not in the book, I think. You saw the match, what the hell could I do? You cannot play better tennis than he did on grass that day.'

If Agassi *v.* Becker had been the high point of the first ten days of the championships, the prospect of a Centre Court semi-final involving the irrepressible Las Vegan and a rejuvenated John McEnroe had connoisseurs positively purring with pleasured anticipation.

McEnroe's role in the metamorphosis of tennis from minority sport to multi-million-dollar industry should never be under-estimated. Ever since the day an eighteen-year-old tousle-haired Irish/American firebrand first picked up his racquet, adjusted his headband, and swaggered off in search of adventure, the noble sport has never been quite the same. The rudest, angriest, brashest and most magnificent teenager the game has ever known came to public notice in 1977 when he romped and stomped his way through the Wimbledon qualifying tournament at Roehampton.

Opponents and officials cowered in submission, and local residents trembled in fear behind their lace curtains as the street sounds of New York rent the genteel air of London SW19. What followed was mayhem on a grand scale. His reign of terror lasted until the semi-finals where he came off second best in a four-set scrap with Jimmy Connors.

Now, in 1992, fifteen years after the devastation caused by that initial visit to Wimbledon, the 33-year-old McEnroe had again reached the round of the last four unseeded after a sequence of heroic victories against Pat Cash, sixteenth-seeded Bollettieri graduate David Wheaton, and the number nine seed Guy Forget of France.

To many, McEnroe remains the most sublimely gifted tennis player of all time, an athlete of true genius who had taken the game on to a new level eight years earlier in 1984 when he won the last of his three Wimbledon finals by routing Connors 6–1, 6–1, 6–2 in front of an incredulous Centre Court audience. In the September of that year, he captured his fourth US Open crown at Flushing Meadow, New York, with another wondrously audacious display, allowing Ivan Lendl just eight games. For one memorable summer McEnroe's tennis was unbeatable, at times virtually unplayable.

The subsequent eight years, sadly, had been a catalogue of suspensions, injuries and ill-timed sabbaticals; of arguments with umpires, of scuffles with photographers, of squandered opportunities, of crazed self-destruction. Sadly, it looked increasingly likely that the man Rod Laver still describes as 'quite possibly the most brilliant talent we will ever see' would be best remembered not for his seven Grand Slam titles, but for being thrown out of the 1990 Australian Open following an insane outburst against Sweden's Mikael Pernfors at Flinders Park, Melbourne.

Just occasionally, however, McEnroe would provide a poignant reminder of what might have been. After three undistinguished years from 1986–8, he reached the Wimbledon semi-finals in 1989, the last four of the 1990 US Open, and the quarter-finals of the Australian Open in January 1992 when he whipped Becker 6–4, 6–3, 7–5 along the way.

Though there are those who will forever dismiss McEnroe as a snarling guttersnipe who debased both himself and sport in general with his petulant tantrums, the private McEnroe is actually quiet, thoughtful, self-effacing, wryly amusing and an indomitable champion of the underdog. The staccato, seemingly disconnected, delivery of his thoughts serves only to reveal the inner torment.

'Deep in my heart I want to give it one more shot. I'm convinced in my own mind I can be as good as I was in 1984. The real tragedy is that when I was number one in the world for all those years I didn't really have the chance to enjoy it. I was never as rough as my exterior suggests.'

Not surprisingly, the fiery Irish New Yorker and the flashy Persian Nevadan had immediately locked horns on first meeting during the World Championship of Tennis (WCT) finals in Dallas in 1989. Agassi defaulted during the second set of their first-round encounter, complaining of a pulled muscle while displaying no discernible signs of a limp. 'His behaviour is bizarre, it's unbelievable,' complained McEnroe at the time, in a blistering attack on the younger man's attitude, which included the words 'immature', 'insulting', and a 'cop-out'. 'People would have respected him more if he'd put in the effort, but it sort of seemed a foregone conclusion that he wasn't going to play.'

The two were finally brought together by American Davis Cup captain Tom Gorman, acting under orders from the United States Tennis Association (USTA), which insisted the two sit down together before that year's quarter-final tie against France in San Diego. According to reliable witnesses, their conversation at a poolside table overlooking Mission Bay went something like this:

Agassi: 'I really don't appreciate some of the things I hear you've been saying, John. I've always searched for good things to say about you, and I don't see as how you're doing the same for me. It appears all you're doing is dwelling on the bad things, the negative side of my character.'

McEnroe: 'Look Andre, people, reporters, whoever, come up to me and say, "Agassi did this, Agassi said that, what do you think?" My reply is, "Well, I don't think that's very good for tennis." It has nothing to do with what I think of you as a person. I like you fine. If you want one piece of advice, never let a newspaper or magazine article get you down. Do me one favour, be a little more open and talk to me about things. Listen to my advice, if you want to.'

Agassi: 'That's a deal. Just don't try and give me any advice through the media.'

Final result: United States 5, France 0, and a lasting if unlikely friendship formed.

At the start of Wimbledon fortnight, London's bookmakers would have offered long odds against Agassi and McEnroe meeting for a place in the final of the 1992 men's singles championship. Leaving aside Agassi's chances of advancement for the moment, world number one Jim Courier, who as winner of the Australian and French Open titles was chasing a possible Grand Slam, 1987 champion Pat Cash, Michael Chang, David Wheaton and Guy Forget were all poised menacingly in McEnroe's quarter of the draw.

But the gods were smiling upon McEnroe that summer. For one thing, the British tabloid press was otherwise engaged in charting the spectacularly unexpected progress of Jeremy Bates, who had caused a first-day sensation by removing Chang in straight sets. By the time the Briton had also accounted for Spaniard Javier Sanchez and Frenchman Thierry Champion, the reluctant hero's name and face were suddenly famous across the land. 'I'd just like to live quietly,' implored the notoriously temperamental Bates during one of his anguished post-match press conferences. 'Don't worry, after this week, you'll be able to do that for the next twenty years,' muttered one onlooker. 'I want to be left alone,' pleaded Solihull's finest. 'Garbo today, garbage tomorrow,' scribbled the man from the *Daily Star* happily.

All four wheels duly fell off the Bates bandwagon in the fourth round as Forget restored French pride by coming back from match point down in the fourth set to win 6–7, 6–4, 3–6, 7–6, 6–3, thereby depriving Britain of its first men's singles quarter-finalist since 1973, when Roger Taylor outlasted a sixteen-year-old Bjorn Borg 6–1, 6–8, 3–6, 6–3, 7–5 on the Centre Court before losing to eventual champion Jan Kodes of Czechoslovakia in the semi-finals.

When Bates drifted off back into the obscurity from whence he had come, the Great British tennis fan immediately found another hero in the unlikely shape of one-time superbrat McEnroe, who had enjoyed a somewhat tempestuous relationship with Wimbledon over the years. His screams of, 'This place is the pits' and, 'You have got to be kidding me' had outraged the crusty membership of the All England Lawn Tennis and Croquet Club. Now a happily married family man, McEnroe was enjoying something of a rehabilitation. The tennis public was gradually, if belatedly, coming to realise that Wimbledon would be a much poorer place when the Great One finally stopped playing.

Thus McEnroe found his every appearance at the 1992 championships accompanied not only by wildly enthusiastic cheering, but with genuine affection. 'I guess they've learned I'm not such a bad guy after all,' said McEnroe, who was both surprised and touched by the warmth of his reception. 'It's a pity I couldn't have enjoyed the same reaction ten years ago, say, but it's nice to be appreciated all the same.'

After an undistinguished opening match on court two, where he struggled to subdue little-known Brazilian Luiz Mattar in four sets, McEnroe produced a vintage display to defeat close friend and regular guitar-plucking partner Pat Cash 6–7, 6–4, 6–7, 6–3, 6–2 in an epic Centre Court contest which held the millions watching on television spellbound for a magical four hours and nine minutes. 'That had to be about the best match I'd played on the Centre Court since I was in the finals all those years,' says McEnroe of that nerve tingling afternoon. 'Beating Pat like that, and the way in which the match was played, is something I'll always be proud of.'

Cash himself was in no doubt that he had been in the company of true magnificence, describing McEnroe as 'the greatest player who has ever walked on a tennis court'. The compliment brought a fleeting smile to the face of the former champion: 'It's just about the most wonderful compliment you can get, isn't it? I guess since he's a good friend Pat might be a little bit biased, but I'd have to say that match will provide a fabulous memory of Wimbledon when I'm no longer around the place.'

As to his prospects of winning a fourth Wimbledon crown, McEnroe was less enthusiastic as he prepared to meet the big-serving Wheaton for a place in the round of the last sixteen: 'Well, I suppose if a couple of the guys fall over and break a leg or something I could go all the way, but you'd have to view me as a long shot.' A straight-set demolition of Wheaton, and a similarly smooth passage against Russian Andrei Olhovsky, who had thrashed world number one and top seed Jim Courier in sensational manner on the Centre Court in the third round, took McEnroe into a potentially hazardous quarter-final with Forget.

The left-handed Frenchman, born in Casablanca and a near-world-championship-standard surfer, wins most of his matches on the strength of an explosive first serve which has lifted him into the top ten on the ATP computer rankings. McEnroe, in irresistible mood, tamed him 6–2, 7–6, 6–3 and now only Agassi stood between him and a sixth appearance in a Wimbledon men's singles final. Did he now regret all the advice and coaching he had passed on to his younger rival?

'No, I don't regret it,' said McEnroe on the dawn of their eagerly awaited Centre Court battle. 'It's great for us both to play here at this stage of the championship. Andre's not that experienced on grass, but the way he plays is so different from the way most guys play on a grass court that it's obviously going to be very tough for me. At thirty-three, it's suddenly like I'm being asked to go toe-to-toe with a twenty-year-old Borg all over again.'

For his part, Agassi was as excited as a skittish schoolboy: 'The only thing that could be better than this is if we were meeting in the finals itself. If I can make the most of this opportunity, this could go down as the single most exciting moment of my career. I don't believe there's one other player in the whole of tennis who's happier for me than John is. If I was to lose, I really couldn't think of anybody I'd rather lose to.'

Like Forget, Agassi spent much of the pre-match build-up explaining what an honour it was to play McEnroe, at Wimbledon, on the Centre Court, and in the semi-finals at that. Though his young opponent spoke with a trace of genuine awe in his voice, McEnroe remained unimpressed: 'I think it's a bit of a gimmick among the newer players. You know, like, "We're all honoured to play him – and we'd like to kick his ass." It's a good notch on their belt, that's all. You think Forget feels honoured right now that I beat him in three straight sets? It's exactly the same situation with Andre. Oh yeah, he's going to be very honoured to play me, but if by some chance I win, he won't be so happy.'

When the talking stopped, Agassi ripped through a one-sided slaughter 6–4, 6–2, 6–3 with another sizzling display of tennis from the back court. The old champion offered flashes of defiance, but his style of tennis, all caresses and gentle nudges, suddenly looked antiquated against Agassi's ferocious attack from the baseline. 'Jimmy Connors was always the guy who returned my serve better than anyone,' said McEnroe at a recent tournament, 'but Andre has taken over that mantle. I'm sure if you ask Boris or Stefan or Courier or whoever they'll all tell you the same thing. Andre's without doubt the best returner in the game right now. Even though I'd been practising day and night with him, what happened at Wimbledon threw my system right off. The guy's passing was incredible, the ball came back at me so fast my system was going crazy.'

The respect now runs deeper than that between mere tennis rivals: 'I've really gotten to like Andre the more I've gotten to know him. He's young, he's real inquisitive and he's very, very smart. He asks good questions and it's nice to have someone you're working with respond so well.'

If Agassi's arrival in the 106th Wimbledon men's singles final was a minor surprise given his previous form on grass, Goran Ivanisevic's advancement came as a shock to many unfamiliar with both his name and talent. His manager Ion Tiriac describes Ivanisevic, who claimed Croatia's first ever Olympic medal when he won bronze at the Barcelona Games last August, as the future of tennis. Traditionalists, reared on the legends of Big Bill Tilden, Fred Perry and Rod Laver, describe him as a nightmare glimpse of the shape of things to come.

Six feet four inches tall with pipe-cleaner legs, Ivanisevic, known as the Leaning Tower of Split, is a human missile-launcher whose first serve has been timed at 137 mph. He can also display wonderful artistry and the waywardness of the prototype McEnroe. His first coach, Hungarian former Davis Cup player Balazs Taroczy, used to send him out on court with the advice: 'Don't spit and don't throw your racquet at anyone.'

Turfed out of the European under-fourteen Junior Championships for the colour of his language, the duration of his tantrums and the distance of his racquet-hurling, Ivanisevic admits: 'My mind, it sometime go away. Maybe it go to the beach, I don't know. So many times I tell myself what I am doing is stupid. I am playing against five, sometimes five thousand, people every match. Fighting with so many people, it's tough to win.'

Always a free spirit, Ivanisevic raised every eyebrow in the world of tennis when he jettisoned the sympathetic Taroczy and employed in his stead Australian Bob Brett, who had just terminated his successful partnership with Boris Becker. These two diverse personalities came together at the Newsweek Champions' Cup in Indian Wells, California, in March 1992 when the Croatian, and not for the first time in his chequered career, simply threw in the towel after losing the first set to Frenchman Fabrice Santoro. Registering a new 'first' in tennis, Ivanisevic actually ran up to the net to congratulate Santoro before the bemused teenager had completed his serve at match point. Brett, a keen disciple of the work ethic, observed: 'It wasn't a very good start.'

Though Brett would like to crack the whip, it is always easy to see who is the boss at any practice session. 'Right, now let's hit a few forehands,' shouts Brett across the net. 'You hit forehand if you want,' mutters the Croatian defiantly, all the while continuing to wallop his favourite two-fisted backhand with gleeful insurrection. 'I not like other players,' explains Ivanisevic needlessly. 'I cannot bottle up my emotions, my thoughts, my beliefs. I cannot be quiet like a Jim Courier. I have to talk to the people, to everybody. I have to answer back.'

Ivanisevic's determination to do things his way led to another major career 'divorce' when he left Mark McCormack's International Management Group (IMG), whose clients range from Arnold Palmer to Luciano Pavarotti to the Vatican. 'Is better with Tiriac. He has two players only, me and Boris. We have good relations because we have same mentality. Balkan.'

Like Ilie Nastase, whose bizarre behavioural patterns he so often emulates (he turned up for the Eurocard Classic in Stuttgart last February with a Mohican haircut), Ivanisevic can display a touch as soft as silk or as heavy-handed as a blacksmith's, depending upon his mood of the moment. In 1990 he reached the semi-finals at Wimbledon as an unseeded teenager, and twelve months later he crashed out in the second round against British part-time professional Nick Brown (world ranked 591) on an outside court. Ivanisevic shrugged and went out on the town while Brown, overwhelmed by Thierry Champion in the next round, went into retirement.

'That first year, I didn't know what it means to be in semi-finals of Wimbledon. Every day it was Christmas time. It seemed I could have whatever I want.' Becker recalls the match with similar wonderment: 'Goran had no idea how nervous he was supposed to feel. He comes out on the Centre Court to play the defending champion for a place in the Wimbledon final and reels off four clean winners to break my serve in the opening game. If he'd stopped to think what he was doing out there his mind would have snapped.'

Up to Wimbledon, 1992 had been a typical year for Ivanisevic. He had lost to Aaron Krickstein in straight sets in the second round of the Australian Open, had beaten Courier and Edberg to triumph in Stuttgart, but had then suffered three embarrassing defeats, against Omar Camporese of Italy, Argentine Christian Miniussi, and, most surprisingly of all, Japanese number one Shuzo Matsuoka in the Stella Artois championship at Queen's Club. Despite his inconsistent form, the Croatian was seeded four places above Agassi, at number eight.

'Is good what happens,' insisted Ivanisevic before his first-round encounter with the fast-rising German Lars Koslowski. 'Last year when I come to Wimbledon I have just won on grass at Manchester and everybody is asking if I have chance. And then I am saying too much, "Yes, now I am ready," and then this Nick Brown come out from nowhere and I am on my way to airport. This year I am not saying anything. I go for Wimbledon like normal guy. One guy out of 128.'

If Ivanisevic was not exactly talking up a storm during the usual pre-Wimbledon hype, the thunder rumbled and the lightning flashed out on court fourteen where Koslowski was left devastated for the loss of seven games, while his vanquished second-round opponent, Mark Woodforde, remarked in his own laconic Australian way: 'Before the match, everyone I knew was advising me just to concentrate on hitting out against his serves, but what they didn't explain was how can you hit what you can't even see. Goran's second serve is faster than most players' first, though looking back I reckon I did win every rally – both of them. The rest of the points weren't rallies, well, not unless you call an ace a rally, that is.'

The Croatian's looming third-round encounter with Switzerland's Marc Rosset, who would later become Olympic champion in Barcelona at Ivanisevic's expense, was not one for the purists. Tennis, a sport of beauty as once played by Ilie Nastase, Manuel Santana and Nicola Pietrangeli, was about to be taken over by the two most powerful servers the game had ever known. It was almost like Robocop *v.* Terminator.

Philippe Chatrier, the thoughtful Frenchman who spent many years as President of the International Tennis Federation (ITF), is not the only individual appalled by the vision of his once-lovely sport being dominated by muscle, which is why he will continue to pursue his dream of making the service ace obsolete with a policy of disarmament. It is the stated ambition of Chatrier, an unashamed and persuasive romantic, to scrap the second serve in what would be the most radical rule change since the net was lowered to three feet over 100 years ago.

'The ace is absolutely contrary to the spirit of the game,' explains Chatrier, with Gallic passion. 'Tennis is a conversation whereas the ace is brute force. It ends the conversation, full stop. The modern player is clearly fitter and stronger than ever before and the dimensions of the court were not drawn up to accommodate him. The easy way out at times is just to go for broke on serve, brute force replacing technique.' In reality, the contest involving Ivanisevic and Rosset, who had admitted that 'without my serve, I am not really a very good player', was not as gruesome as most had feared, the inventive Croatian punctuating his now customary haul of brutal service winners with some delightfully disguised lobs and subtly angled volleys. 'Is good people see I can play this game, that I know what to do when ball come back at me. I feel comfortable here.

Perhaps, though it is a big perhaps, I reach semi-finals again this time.'

To do so, however, Ivanisevic would have to dispose of two of Wimbledon's favourite adopted sons, Ivan Lendl and Stefan Edberg.

Like Nastase and Rosewall before him, Lendl's record at the All England Club was one of heroic failure. Twice runner-up (to Becker and Cash), five times a losing finalist, the Czechoslovakian-born naturalised American was giving the championships one last superhuman effort at the age of thirty-two and the whole of Britain was firmly behind him. Ivanisevic knew better than most where the sympathy of the crowd lay, for there could be no doubt a triumphant Lendl would be Wimbledon's most cherished champion since his countryman Jaroslav Drobny (and his trusty Dunlop Maxply) triumphed in baggy shorts, beaming smile and spectacles in 1954.

The mystery of grass had long confounded Lendl, reared on the ponderous clay courts of Prague, where he learned to tenderise opponents into submission with his clubbing groundstrokes without ever being called upon to develop the volleying prowess demanded by Wimbledon. Despite many years of intense practice under the expert eye of Tony Roche, one of the finest serve-volleyers ever to come out of Australia, Lendl was no nearer mastering the intricacies of grass. 'If I had a volley half as good as Tony's it would probably be enough,' was his frequent lament.

Though his name is now likely to remain a cruel omission from the roll of honour at the All England Club, Lendl neither needs nor desires our sympathy. He possesses eight Grand Slam titles (two Australian, three French and three US Opens), and has accumulated over $20 million in prize money alone. The last of those eight major championships was achieved at Flinders Park, Melbourne, back in 1990. This time he quit through injury while trailing Ivanisevic 7–6, 1–6, 4–6, 0–1 in what had been an enthralling fourth-round Wimbledon encounter.

'I not like to win this way, but what can I do?' asked Ivanisevic rhetorically. 'For long time he is best player in the world, no question. He still one of toughest opponents mentally, but maybe the body becomes weaker after so many years.' Even a twenty-year-old body finds it hard to withstand the daily grind of the tennis circuit at times, as the Croatian had discovered when he was forced to withdraw from the Monte Carlo Open in the spring of 1992 due to what was later diagnosed as an irregular heartbeat. 'I was scared in the beginning, but they said it was nothing serious. They did a lot of checking and said it was some kind of stress that could affect any sportsman. They said there was no problem and I could continue to play tennis. Now I only have bad back to worry me.'

Where Lendl is a disciple of that popular belief among many Europeans that grass is fit only for cows, Stefan Edberg, Ivanisevic's quarter-final foe, might have been reared on the stuff. Twice champion of Wimbledon, the graceful Swede had been earmarked for true greatness from 1983, when he had completed a teenage 'Grand Slam' at the age of seventeen by winning the junior singles events at all four major championships on three different surfaces: the Australian Open (hard), French Open (clay), Wimbledon (grass) and the US Open (hard). Uniquely in tennis, the Lean Machine, as he is popularly known in the women's locker room, cultivates a low-key off-court image.

On day nine of the 1992 championships, however, the man his British coach Tony Pickard describes as a 'street fighter' was mugged. In complete contradiction of most expert opinion, Edberg wilted in the face of Ivanisevic's ferocious onslaught, even though the Swede won a marvellously competitive first set tie-break 12–10. By the time dusk had fallen, so too had Edberg, by a score of 6–7, 7–5, 6–1, 3–6, 6–3. Thirty-three clean aces took the Croatian's running total to 133 in five matches, and now only American Pete Sampras threatened to interrupt his serene passage to a first Grand Slam final.

'This time different,' explained Ivanisevic. 'First time in semi-finals I came on court like I was going to the pictures. It was good fun, you know, like when you watch good movie. I watch Becker and I watch myself, but I never think I can win. But now I am not getting so crazy, I believe I can win.' And in a poignant reference to the civil war which was ravaging his former homeland of Yugoslavia, he added: 'Also, now I am not only fighting for myself, but for all the people of Croatia. Pete is nice man, but he must not get in my way.' Ivanisevic was also at pains to pay tribute to the influence Brett had exerted to bring about his sudden change of personality. 'He talk to me, he make me see how I complain too much and fight too little. When I watched video of old matches I see this guy from another planet. My coach he tell me I have to change if I want to go forward. Now I am normal guy.'

Though Agassi professed publicly that he was looking no further than his own semi-final against McEnroe, he privately admitted that, should he reach the final, he would rather face the fragile genius of Ivanisevic than his American Davis Cup team-mate Sampras, from whom he had prised a mere nine games in the final of the 1990 US Open at Flushing Meadow. Sampras had arrived at the All England Club last June itching to achieve what was denied his alter-ego Pancho Gonzales by the long delay in the arrival of 'open tennis' and to fulfil his stated boyhood ambition of 'joining the all-time greats'.

The summer of 1992 was not to see the fulfilment of that childhood fantasy, however, for while Sampras took the first set of his semi-final after a tense tie-break, Ivanisevic won a strangely subdued affair 6–7, 7–6, 6–4, 6–2. Perhaps nerves accounted for the poor quality of the match, but perhaps it was the oddness of playing a men's semi-final on court one on what was women's final day (the scheduled programme had been washed out on the Friday afternoon, hence a 24-hour delay), or perhaps it was because both players knew the crowd on number one court was far more interested in the outcome of the

Agassi–McEnroe semi-final being played on the Centre Court. 'It certainly didn't feel like I thought a Wimbledon semi-final was supposed to feel,' murmured Sampras.

No matter the manner of his victory, Ivanisevic was suitably ecstatic. 'I went out to win. Even when I lose first set to Pete I believe I can win. Tomorrow is same,' said the victor, who bagged another thirty-six aces to take his running total for the fortnight to 169. 'I never keep my mind as well so long, so I am very pleased. I have one more day then I can relax my mind for a week, a month maybe. I play Agassi twice last year on slow surfaces and win because he could not break my serve. I know he doesn't like to play me too much. He did not return very well the balls I was serving those two times. If he does return well, maybe I do something crazy, maybe I start serving with right arm, yes?'

On the subject of his suspect back, Ivanisevic was equally flippant: 'It is okay, I think – I hope. I mean I am serving a lot of aces so my back is good. I cannot complain. It is little sore but I no care. Tomorrow is big final. With sore or broken back you go in and that's it. I know Olympics in Barcelona special to people of Croatia, but Wimbledon is my special dream.'

So saying, Ivanisevic departed to continue his recently acquired superstition of eating the same meal at the same table in the same Italian restaurant in Wimbledon High Street every night of the championships: fish soup, fillet of lamb and French fries, and vanilla ice-cream with chocolate sauce topping. 'The waiter – always same one – does not show me menu any more, he just brings food to table as soon as he see me,' he grinned boyishly. And on that same Saturday night before the men's singles final, Agassi, after chomping his way through a 12 oz cheeseburger, was dreaming wondrous dreams of his own. After a 'perfect night's sleep', over breakfast Bollettieri maintained a running one-way conversation delivered in a near-whisper: 'Andre, this is your time. You're so strong now. Your mind is strong, and your body is strong. Remember

Borg. They said he couldn't win from the back court and he won Wimbledon five times. Look what you did to Becker, to McEnroe. No one can live with you if you don't want them to. This is the day, this is your day. The day Andre Agassi becomes a legend.'

Before his final practice, and long before the vast crowds had assembled outside the Fred Perry Gates, Agassi strolled through the still-deserted grounds of the All England Club past the entrance to the Centre Court where the old clock is forever nudging the stroke of two in the mind's eye. While the last furious preparations were being completed inside the stadium, the making ready of the Royal Box, one final polish of the trophy, a scrupulous inspection of the entire court, ensuring the fridges which hold the tennis balls and the players' drinks were full, Agassi slipped away to his favourite private spot by the outside courts looking out to the church spire shimmering in the far-off distance among the mighty oaks and beeches on Wimbledon Hill.

As he took in the scene, Agassi allowed his thoughts to drift back to those early days of turmoil and financial hardship in Las Vegas, to the hours spent hitting tennis balls back to his father, to the years of effort and strife at Bollettieri's, to the victories and to the defeats, and to three other mornings such as this which were to end in defeat and abject misery. 'I knew I couldn't allow myself to fail. Not a fourth time. Another defeat and I realised I would probably commit career suicide.' Bollettieri was less troubled: 'He'd been through it all before. Now he was bigger, stronger and better prepared than ever before. The three other finals were meaningless.'

But Sampras, who knew both finalists' strengths and weaknesses better than most, remembers being rather less certain than Bollettieri about the likely outcome. 'Looking back, I'm not surprised Andre won, though there is no doubt he must have been under more pressure than Goran. It was Goran's first major final and he knew that whatever happened there

163

would be others. What you had was the best server ['Serve, serve, serve. Forty aces. Win. Boring,' is how Ivanisevic often describes his game with heavy irony] against the best returner. It was such a big moment in their lives, I wasn't surprised when one of them finally cracked.'

But before the Croatian buckled and Agassi ended his long, long wait to gain what was not just a major prize but the biggest prize of all, winning 6–7, 6–4, 6–4, 1–6, 6–4, the two finalists traded blows for two hours fifty minutes in what will undoubtedly be remembered as one of the most exciting Centre Court matches of the modern era. After Ivanisevic secured a nail biting 41-minute opening set following an eighteen-point tie-break, Agassi produced some of the most inspired tennis to take the next two sets, before a serious lapse in concentration allowed Ivanisevic to square the match and force a climactic fifth set.

'But even after I'd lost that first set when Goran hit a stupendous ace with his second serve on set point, I was still supremely confident. I suppose I'd half-expected to go into the match feeling "I hope I don't lose again" rather than "I'm going to win this time", but I really felt no tension. All I could feel was ability. I felt I was overflowing with ability, that I could hit any shot I wanted. In the fourth and fifth sets Goran was serving so big, bigger than he did in the very first game even, that I would have had to tip my hat to him if he'd kept it up. Even if he had, though, I was determined to hang on in there and wait for any chance that might come my way. I knew I might only get the one chance, so I was determined one would be enough.'

If Agassi was going to fold as he had done in his three previous Grand Slam finals, it would surely be now, as the pressure intensified in the fifth set, but at 3–3, 30–40, and with defeat a distinct possibility, he produced a daring second serve followed by the bravest volley he had ever executed. From deuce he then won the next two points with ease and the danger was past. As the set progressed, so Agassi began performing with even greater accuracy, power and boldness. Suddenly, at 4–5, the Croatian's seemingly bottomless well of aces dried up at 37 for the day and a remarkable 206 for the championship. The 1992 Wimbledon final was about to take one final, dramatic twist. Ivanisevic's serve, the most potent weapon in the game, was to become the very instrument of his own downfall.

One dismal double fault was followed by another, 0–30. 'I couldn't allow myself to think "This is it" at that precise moment, but I do remember whispering "This could be it",' relives Agassi. 'When you've been through all the disappointments I'd been through – the two French finals against Gomez and Courier, the US Open against Sampras – you hesitate a little bit before allowing yourself to feel that you're on the very edge of victory. Never forget the old saying, "It ain't over till the fat lady sings." Well, at 4–5, 0–30, I couldn't even hear the fat lady humming yet. Instead of serving two doubles, Goran might just as easily have ripped two aces past me and been 30–0 up. He could still find four clean aces in a row from somewhere, as he'd done before, and it would have been five-all in games and I'd have been left wondering whether I'd just blown a fourth Grand Slam.'

Agassi's misgivings were fully justified. Following those two nervous double faults, another service flew well wide before Ivanisevic finally found the target for the first time in six attempts in that decisive tenth game with a second service which clipped the very outside of the centre line in a puff of chalk dust and flew off the rim of the American's outflung racquet. It was 15–30. Another service winner by the Croatian took the score to 30–30, but he was then left stranded flat-footed in mid-court when the Las Vegan stepped forward to unleash the latest in a long series of flashing forehand winners. 30–40. Championship point.

Seen through Ivanisevic's eyes, the climax offers the perfect illustration of the painfully sharp contrast between victory and defeat: 'Was little bit rushing,' recalls the Croatian of his first nerve-riddled serve on match point. 'I throw ball too high. Was looking for ball. Was thinking too much. I don't know where to hit it, his forehand or backhand. I lose motion. I miss. Second serve, no good. Is sitting up like little dog begging. Next thing I know the other guy is down on the floor. Oh, no. Unbelievable. I lose Wimbledon. That's it. Over.'

Agassi's emotions tumbled around in similar disarray as Ivanisevic's final shot hit the net. At last he was a champion, and not just any champion; the champion of Wimbledon, like Spencer W. Gore, the first champion in 1877, like Bill Tilden, Donald Budge, Fred Perry, Rod Laver, Bjorn Borg and John McEnroe. 'I was . . . oh, I don't know, shocked, I suppose. I was completely overwhelmed. I wish I could have had a video of my mind at that very second because my memory of what exactly happened after Goran's volley failed to clear the net is still very hazy. I didn't have time to think, "I can't believe it, he's missed it, I've won Wimbledon." All I was thinking was, "It's over, it's over, it's over."

'If I'd lost, I suppose I would have started thinking about quitting tennis altogether. Really, I'd have felt that down. It took a great effort to reach the finals, and it took another great effort to keep playing as well as I was right into a fifth set. Suddenly, after all the years of work, and hopes, and doubts, and prayers, it's match point. Crunch time. In a few minutes you will either walk off that court – and with the whole world watching you – feeling better than you have ever felt in your life before, or feeling worse than you could ever imagine. It was a dramatic moment for me. I needed that title and I needed it badly. Nick needed it and my father needed it. I also think my fans needed it because they had to have a reason to keep believing. Then there were my critics. They needed a little dose of reality, that not only can I actually play this game, but that I can be a winner.'

For Agassi's many critics, it was a time of sober reassessment. The young Las Vegan had finally proved he was a champion first and a billboard second. 'You know, I'd never been in any doubts as to why I was in tennis. It's difficult coming into any sport as a sixteen-year-old and worse if overnight you've become popular and are being presented as something of a celebrity. To a large degree, I think sections of the media and the public imagined I was deliberately concocting the whole image thing. So no one listened when I tried to explain, "Look, you're giving me way too much credit. I wish I was that smart that I could sort of invent myself."

'I knew what I wanted. I always knew what was really inside me, even if a lot of other people chose to ignore my tennis and concentrate on my hair, or my clothes, or the way I acted sometimes on court. But I think the emotion I showed after winning Wimbledon revealed to everyone what it meant to me. Looking back, I believe it was one of those magical moments in sport where the fans can actually identify with the athlete, feel exactly what the athlete is feeling. The people who hark back to the "image is everything" thing don't understand what I'm about. I'll rephrase that. They don't want to understand me.'

And so on that sunny Sunday evening in July 1992, Agassi, accompanied by girlfriend Wendy Stewart and coach Nick Bollettieri, was driven through the cheering crowds, past the statue of Fred Perry and out the front gates of the All England Club that he had once so detested. As his chauffeur-driven limousine climbed Wimbledon Hill Road towards their rented house on Wimbledon Common, Agassi watched the scene of his triumph slowly disappear from view out of the rear window before turning to the man sitting at his side, where he had been for nine years.

'Wimbledon, Nick. I never realised what it all meant. Nothing, and I mean nothing, compares with winning Wimbledon – except maybe winning it again next year.'

After the Dream

Just two years after Agassi's brief flirtation with greatness on the Centre Court at Wimbledon in 1992, most of the old crowd are gone now. As the champion's weight, fitness and commitment to the daily grind of the men's tennis circuit continue to fluctuate alarmingly, so the members of the entourage have each drifted slowly away to find more appreciative companions.

Wendy Stewart finally gave up trying to comprehend the whims of the emotional butterfly sometimes to be found at her side, though the two remain 'good friends'. Bill Shelton declined to follow his guv'nor to Nevada when Agassi announced he was moving the running of his entire business empire to Las Vegas. Nike, fearing they had already seen the best of their vastly expensive clothes-horse, shelled out many extra millions to persuade the increasingly dominant Sampras and Courier to further the glory of the corporate logo. Nick Bollettieri, almost inevitably, grew weary of watching his fabulous creation go through life with his finger permanently poised over the self-destruct button.

Ever one for a new challenge, Bollettieri undertook the task of rebuilding the crumbling career of another fragile champion,

Boris Becker. (Becker had been trapped in a spiralling decline ever since winning the last of his five major championships at the 1991 Australian Open in Melbourne.) 'Spiritually, Andre will always be like a son to me,' said Bollettieri with genuine sadness at the parting. 'But maybe we had become too close. Maybe our lives had become so entangled we could inflict too much hurt upon each other. Maybe it is just time Andre Agassi learned to take responsibility for his own actions.'

For Agassi, the past two years have been characteristically traumatic; content with his role of global celebrity, he has slidden inexorably down the world rankings and his appearances on the tennis court (with a few honourable exceptions) have been a miserable disappointment to those who believe a Wimbledon champion bears a special responsibility every time he or she picks up a racquet in earnest.

In his very first match after that Centre Court triumph against Goran Ivanisevic, Agassi succumbed with not even the semblance of a fight against the veteran American Kevin Curren in Washington, before collecting the Canadian Open in Toronto with a three-set demolition of Ivan Lendl, winning 3-6, 6-2, 6-0. Since that effort back in July 1992, however, he has managed to win just two more titles: both second division ATP Tour events at San Francisco and Scottsdale.

Like some ageing boxing champ who, having cashed in his title, is more than happy to serve as a human punch-bag for those hungry warriors on the way up, the one-time wizard of Wimbledon has suffered a catalogue of depressing defeats: Peruvian Jaime Yzaga; Nicklas Kulti of Sweden; Patrick Kuhnen from Germany; former Davis Cup colleague Brad Gilbert; Switzerland's Marc Rosset; Dutchman Richard Krajicek; Spain's Sergi Bruguera; Carl-Uwe Steeb, yet again; Aaron Krickstein; new American hope Todd Martin (twice); Michael Chang; Russian Andrei Medvedev; Thomas Enqvist, the latest Swedish sensation. They have all claimed his prized scalp. In the 15 months between Wimbledon 1992 and the

1993 US Open, Agassi played 61 singles matches, winning 44 (against, almost without exception, moderate opposition) and losing 17.

Yet Agassi has still found time to provide the tingle of excitement, the sense of theatre, the kind of magic of which only he is capable. Whilst a succession of great names from tennis's recent golden past, most notably John Newcombe, have bemoaned the lack of personality displayed by Sampras, Courier and their poe-faced ilk, Agassi, for good or bad, has seldom been out of the headlines or newspaper gossip columns for long.

As befits an inveterate hogger of limelights, he has kept his best (and, some critics would say, his worst) only for those occasions when he could feel the eyes of the world upon him. After outplaying Stefan Edberg in a crucial singles match during the United States' defeat of Sweden in the semi-finals of the 1992 Davis Cup competition, Agassi and his cocky American team-mates unexpectedly found themselves confronted by lowly Switzerland in the final. Only the combination of John McEnroe and his easily-influenced young cohort could have whipped up the 'Let's Kick Ass' atmosphere which greeted Jakob Hlasek and Marc Rosset that pre-Christmas weekend in Fort Worth, Texas.

Agassi opened the contest by overwhelming Hlasek 6-1, 6-2, 6-2 then called for McEnroe to be appointed US Davis Cup captain in place of the incumbent Tom Gorman. Not that he was issuing an ultimatum to the USTA, you understand. Only that 'John could be the difference between my playing and not playing in the future.'

Agassi's threats were received with indignation at the USTA (which would later name Tom Gullikson as Gorman's successor) and what had appeared to be the most mundane of Davis Cup finals suddenly erupted into open warfare after Rosset had levelled the tie at 1-1 with a stunning five-set victory over Courier. The unthinkable, a Swiss triumph, then become a distinct possibility when Hlasek and Rosset took a two-set lead over McEnroe and a visibly shell-shocked Sampras in the doubles.

In the words of the normally placid Sampras, McEnroe proceeded to 'go ape-shit'. He abused officials, complained about the Swiss supporters' infernal cow-bells, then ripped off his shirt and threw it into the frenzied crowd to celebrate winning the third set. Agassi, for his part, beat his fists upon the advertising boards around the perimeter of the court and screamed at one bell-clanging spectator, 'If you're Swiss . . . you can kiss my ass.' After McEnroe and Sampras recovered to win in five torrid sets (Courier then defeated Hlasek for overall victory), an unrepentant Agassi observed, 'That's what the Davis Cup is all about. You root for the goodies, and holler at the baddies.'

If the old year had ended in a somewhat typical fashion, 1993 began in depressingly familiar style when Agassi opted out of the Australian Open for the seventh successive time. Whilst Courier was going about the business of amassing his fourth Grand Slam crown, his life-long rival was content to bask in the Las Vegas sun before making his seasonal debut at San Francisco in early February, beating Brad Gilbert in the final for the eighteenth title of his career.

Though his nineteenth title was to follow swiftly at Scottsdale, Agassi quickly disappeared from public view after losing to Bruguera in the quarter-finals of the Barcelona Open in April, claiming tendonitis of the right wrist. Amid rumours that Agassi would not only miss the forthcoming French Open but also the 1993 Wimbledon Championships, he reappeared in Paris at the end of May to participate in a bizarre but carefully stage-managed press conference held before a mainly family audience at a chic Paris sports club. 'Interviewed' by his buddy McEnroe, Agassi let slip an ill-timed *double entendre* with regards to what he could and could no longer do with his injured right hand, and offered an unnecessarily offensive remark concerning Sampras, suggesting the new world number one looked as though he had only recently swung down from a tree.

It was only Sampras's gracious acceptance of Agassi's grudging and belated apology which marked the end of this sorry affair unbefitting a Wimbledon hero. Yet as Bruguera pounded his way past Courier to become the first Spaniard to win the French Open since Andres Gimeno in 1972, there could be no doubting just who was the real start of the show in Paris.

Agassi's standing in the grand scheme of things had been made abundantly clear during an Elton John concert held at the start of the tournament in the Palais Bercy. As the then-reigning Wimbledon champion, always more Rod Stewart than Rod Laver in dress and demeanour, swaggered into the pyramid-style arena, he was greeted with an ecstatic roar of acclaim by an audience already sated by the non-stop parade of celebrities. In decibels alone, Agassi's entrance drowned out anything that had gone before, including the arrival of actress-singer Vanessa Paradis and France's soccer heart-throb Michel Platini.

Indeed, so renowned had Agassi become, that even in his home town of Las Vegas, where celebrities just about outnumber the slot-machines, the Nevada Kid attracts attention wherever he goes. 'Listen to what I'm telling you,' drawls Dave Sorensen, head barman at the Mirage Hotel. 'We've had everyone in the world walk through here. Well, everyone in the world who is anyone, if you know what I'm saying. Frank Sinatra, Diana Ross, we've even had Michael Jackson, right? The only time those slots were abandoned, instantly, was when Agassi breezed in. He's still mobbed on sight.'

And so the tennis circus moved on to Wimbledon. But with or without the blonde one? As founder, chairman and chief executive officer of Nike, Phil Knight is one of the few people alive who can hope to exert any influence over the company's wayward mannequin. 'He'll be there. I really believe Andre will defend his title on that opening Monday if he has to be carried onto the Centre Court. He has told me he'll play even if he has to receive pain-killing injections for his injured wrist. And Andre invariably means what he says.'

Agassi himself playfully fuelled the mystery surrounding the seriousness of his injury by leading interviewers to believe he had not so much as hit a ball in 10 weeks, that he would not be able to practice until the week before Wimbledon began, and that if he did show up at the All England Club, it would be because of his love of the place rather than any expectancy of victory.'Bullshit,' revealed a Nike insider. 'Our Andre has been practising like billy-o with McEnroe on a grasscourt in Newport, Rhode Island.'

Whatever the truth, Agassi's long-awaited re-emergence actually took place the week before Wimbledon at Halle in Germany when he was easily outplayed on grass by Steeb, that by now frequent irritant. The mob of media hounds who accompanied him on that venture were united in their disdain. The reigning champion was overweight, grossly unfit, lacking match practice, bereft of motivation, and totally unable to stage a meaningful defence.

When the first-round Wimbledon draw paired him with the fast-emerging young German Bernd Karbacher, so-called expert opinion predicted Agassi would become the first defending champion to be defeated in the opening round since Manuel Santana of Spain lost to Charlie Pasarell in 1967. In short, Karbacher was the perfect champ-basher. No matter, the adoring crowds turned up in their thousands to greet the returning champion with a tumultuous welcome.

'We feed off each other,' said Agassi of the Wimbledon faithful before walking out to meet Karbacher. 'They love to have me and I just love to be here.' Result? Game, set and match Agassi 7-5, 6-4, 6-0 and the unmistakable sound of egg yolk being wiped from a thousand faces.

Though discernibly puffier around the waist and thighs than the whippet-like athlete of 12 months earlier, Agassi was not only remarkably fleet-footed for one who had not 'lifted a racquet' in 10 weeks, but had acquired a newly-designed service action which, according to leading coach and former Wimbledon doubles champion Dennis Ralston, 'must have taken months to perfect.'

But why discuss Agassi's tennis when there were far more important issues abroad? His on-off (on-again, off-again) romance with 'la Streisand' proved of great interest to the press, not to mention his total lack of body hair which, compared to the hirsute model of old, made him look like some alien from Dr. Who in the eyes of Fleet Street's notorious Beastie Boys.

If he was fleshier, he was also funnier with tabloid inquisitors than ever before. *Have you shaved your body hair, Andre?* 'I guess you could say that.' *Could you tell us why?* 'It makes me a little more aerodynamic out there.' *What method did you use to remove it?* 'There are times, depending on what the other options are, when I have to do it myself. Sometimes, I'll have someone else do it. But I'm very selective . . . put it this way, I wouldn't let you do it.'

Grilled about his relationship with Streisand, who arrived on the Centre Court amid an electrical storm of flashbulbs in time to see her friend lose a thrilling five-setter to eventual champion Sampras in the quarter-finals, Agassi offered us a rare insight into his real personality. 'I'm never offended by such intrusions into my private life by the press. After all, 50 per cent of the time I'm only humouring them. It's just harmless fun.'

Though the remainder of 1993 was to bring a succession of disappointments (particularly a first round defeat by Enqvist at the US Open), Agassi has no intentions of entering the rest home for faded champions. Thus the early months of 1994 were spent preparing for the only tournament which really matters.

'Most places I go, 20 to 30 per cent of the crowd will go out of their way to cheer the other guy, so Wimbledon is something incredible. I know a lot of people are sceptical of me and wonder if I'm sincere. They may have a better perspective on me in Britain. Don't forget it was there, on one Sunday afternoon I fulfilled a life-long dream. And those people saw it . . . they've seen a side of me a lot of others haven't.'

Index